D1148667

Best Courses in Scotland

Best Courses in
SCOTLAND

AURUM PRESS

First published in Great Britain 2000
by Aurum Press Ltd, 25 Bedford Avenue, London WC1B 3AT

Copyright © 2000 by EMAP Publications

All rights reserved. No part of this book may be reproduced or utilized in any
form or by any means, electronic or mechanical, including photocopying,
recording or by any information storage and retrieval system, without prior
permission from Aurum Press Ltd.

A catalogue record for this book is available from the British Library.

ISBN 1 85410 683 X

1 3 5 7 9 10 8 6 4 2
2000 2002 2004 2003 2001

Text compiled and written by Jim Humberstone and Bill Robertson
Design by Don Macpherson
Typeset by Action Publishing Technology Ltd, Gloucester
Printed and bound in Great Britain by
CPD Group, Wales

Contents

Foreword by Bill Robertson   vii

Preface by Steve Prentice   ix

Introduction   1

Top 20 Courses   4

10 Best Value Courses   5

10 Most Difficult Courses   6

Top 10 Courses for Welcome   7

Star Ratings   8

Course Listings   11

Index   113

Foreword

With golf, as with life, one man's meat is, more often than not, another man's poison – especially when it comes to defining exactly what constitutes a good golf course.

For many golfers the historic links courses are the oldest, most traditional and therefore quite obviously the best. Other players, however, will argue with equal conviction that nothing can match the quiet tranquility and scenic beauty of playing the game on a mature and superbly manicured inland layout. Whatever your golfing preference, you are sure to be spoiled for choice by this great new book, which provides a comprehensive list of 200 recommended golf courses covering the length and breadth of Scotland. As well as all the essential information from green fees to visitor restrictions, you'll also learn about the best, and worst, holes; the speed of the greens; the depth of the rough and the type of terrain each course is laid out over. You can even discover exactly how friendly the natives are!

Many of the most famous golfing venues, both seaside and inland, are bound to be on your own 'must play' list of courses. But *Best Courses in Scotland* also includes a host of smaller hidden gems which you can now look forward to discovering – golf courses that more often than not boast outstanding and wonderfully scenic layouts, offer great value for money and always afford the golfing visitor the warmest of welcomes. And because all the courses featured have also been assessed by *Golf World* readers, you will be able to discover what your fellow amateur golfers have to say about them.

Bill Robertson

Preface

Welcome to *Golf World's Best Courses in Scotland*. For those of you who enjoy discovering new and exciting courses to play, this book offers the ultimate guide to some of the best-value golf to be found anywhere in the world. It has been created especially to provide readers with the essential information required to fully enjoy the wide diversity, outstanding quality and unique character of the golf courses which make Scotland such a popular golfing destination. Each of the 200 courses included has been individually rated by readers and members of *Golf World* staff on providing an overall golfing experience, by highlighting such things as: quality and difficulty of the courses, the clubhouse facilities, value for money and the friendliness – or otherwise – of the welcome you can expect. In this book we have deliberately made judgements about the courses included, to provide considerably more information about the golf clubs you may consider visiting than simply the green fee, the par of the course, the address and the secretary's phone number.

Golf World's 1000 Best Golf Courses in Britain and Ireland, which was published in 1999, has already proved to be an outstanding success. This new book expands and refines this winning formula by providing the same detailed information, along with personal comments, on 200 Scottish golf courses. Some of the courses are better than others. There are those which are less challenging but outstandingly scenic, while others provide as tough and demanding a test as you will find anywhere the game of golf is played. But the one thing all the 200 courses featured have in common is the fact that they have each been subjected to *Golf World's* detailed evaluation.

Whether you intend to visit the Scottish courses featured with a couple of regular playing partners from your local golf club, or as a member of a larger, more organised golf society, this book will help you make the right choice. To enable you to plan your visit more easily, the book has been divided into Scotland's recognised golfing regions. Separate listings have also been given to highlight the most friendly and best value clubs, and for each region we also spotlight our favourite course, or courses. So whether you are the kind of golfer who enjoys the scenery as much as the golfing challenge, or a committed player keen to test your skills against the very best Scotland has to offer, we trust you will find everything you are looking for in this new *Golf World* book.

Steve Prentice
Editor, *Golf World*

Introduction

Golf World launched its first nationwide survey of Scottish golf courses in October 1999. Through our readers, we aimed to produce the first independent, authoritative guide to the best golf courses to play. The rankings and ratings contained in this book completely reflect the thoughts and experiences of ordinary golfers.

Lists of the best places to play are typically selected by professionals, course designers and figures of authority within the golfing industry. Unlike the golfing cognoscenti, who are not out there playing courses day in, day out, the green-fee-paying golfer is, and is often better placed to identify the strengths and weaknesses of the top courses.

Upon this premise, we asked our readers to evaluate 200 preselected courses in four different categories: value for money, course difficulty, quality of welcome and overall rating.

By ranking the courses in these categories, we aimed to answer questions that the typical golfer might ask before visiting a new course. Is it worth the money? Is the course too hard for a player of my standard? Where will I be made welcome? We also wanted to know what, in the opinion of the grass-roots golfers, were the best courses in Scotland.

While the ratings and rankings achieved the purpose of grading each course, we also wanted golfers' comments about them. At the foot of each entry in this guide you will find individual comments about the 200 courses from the people who have played them – in many cases the comments are as illuminating as the ratings.

Any guide that attempts to grade courses is open to criticism. People like different courses for different reasons. We are acutely aware of this fact and have tried to balance the ratings and comments to achieve a fair, rational view. Hopefully you will agree. If not, it should cause a lively debate in the club bar, and we welcome any views or comments you should have about this guide.

How to use this guide

This book has been divided into three sections for quick and easy reference. In the first section you will find the following rankings: the Top 20 Courses, the 10 Best Value Courses, the 10 Most Difficult Courses and the Top 10 Courses for Welcome.

In the second section are the star ratings for all 200 courses, rated from five star to one star as follows:

★★★★★ – Exceptional. The best.
★★★★ – Excellent. An outstanding day's golf.
★★★ – Very good.
★★ – Good, but not great.
★ – Standard – nothing special.

The third section is the main part of the book, listing all 200 Scottish courses featured. Here you will find all the information you need to organise a game. The listing covers each of the Scottish regions, and a review of Golf World's favourite course (or courses) in the region appears at the beginning of each regional listing.

This is a typical entry:

Blairgowrie Golf Club (Rosemount)   ★★★★

Rosemount, Blairgowrie, PH10 6LG
Nearest main town: Perth

Secretary:	Mr. J. N. Simpson	Tel: 01250 872 622
		Fax: 01250 875451
Professional:	Mr. C. Dernie	Tel: 01259 873116
		Fax: 10250 873116

Playing: Midweek: round £50.00; day £60.00. Weekend: round £55.00: day £75

Facilities: Bar: 11am–11pm. Food: Lunch and dinner from 10am–9pm. Bar snacks.

Comments: Setting and presentation could not be better ... Generally overrated ... Unique in Scotland but not a patch on Sunningdale, Liphook, Swinley Forest, West Sussex ... Expensive with poor visitor facilities ... If I lived in Scotland this would be the club I would join ... Visitors are not made to feel welcome ... Unique in Scotland ... Each hole is separate from the others ... Great flora and fauna.

– The information listed is accurate at the time of going to press. The bar and catering times given are expected opening times during the summer. In many cases during the winter, bar and catering times are likely to be shorter due to the early close of play.

– There are four possible green fee prices for weekday round/day and weekend round/day. Where there is no price next to an entry, it means that price is not available at the club. Although we have indicated the most recent prices quoted prior to going to press, green fees can change during the course of the year. Check with the golf club prior to your visit.

Advice for Visitors

It often feels as though you need a special handshake to get into some golf courses, and some clubs tend to be protective of their courses, much as a child guards his or her favourite toy. Provided you are a bona fide golfer and are clear on golf etiquette, you only require a few simple rules to smooth the way.

The majority of the courses listed in the book require visitors to contact the club in advance and some may also ask you to produce a handicap certificate on the day of play. That is normally sufficient. When approaching some of the more exclusive courses, it is recommended that you also write a letter of introduction direct to the secretary or organise a letter of introduction from your own club secretary.

With the exception of a very few clubs, there is nothing to stop you playing the best courses in the country, provided you follow these basic introductions. If you do not have a handicap, then the best advice is to follow the normal procedures and hope for the best – you may be asked to prove your ability when you arrive at the club.

Clubs have many competition and society days during the year, so find out the best days for visitors before you go. If you turn up on the door, you may be disappointed. Also, men should remember to pack a jacket and tie as many clubs have a dress code in the bar and dining room.

Good golfing!

TOP 20 COURSES

1.   Muirfield
2.   St Andrews (Old)
3.   Royal Dornoch
4.   Carnoustie (Championship)
5.   Turnberry (Ailsa)
6.   Cruden Bay
7   Royal Aberdeen
8.   Royal Troon
9.   Loch Lomond
10   Glasgow Gailes
11.   The Roxburghe
12.   Montrose Medal
13   Southerness
14.   Prestwick
15.   Blairgowrie (Rosemount)
16.   Gleneagles
17.   Nairn
18   Ladybank
19.   Boat of Garten
20.   Kingsbarns

10 BEST VALUE COURSES

1. Boat of Garten
2. Southerness
3. Dunbar
4. Cruden Bay
5. Machrihanish
6. Belleisle
7. St Andrews (New)
8. Nairn
9. Crieff
10. Ladybank

10 MOST DIFFICULT COURSES

1.   Carnoustie
2.   Turnberry (Ailsa)
3.   Muirfield
4.   Royal Troon
5.   Western Gailes
6.   Royal Dornoch
7.   St. Andrews (Old Course)
8.   Machrihanish
9.   The Roxburghe
10. Cruden Bay

TOP 10 COURSES FOR WELCOME

1.   Duff House Royal
2.   Loch Lomond
3.   Machire Hotel
4.   Western Gailes
5.   Dumfries & Country
6.   Crail
7.   Kilspindie
8.   Royal Dornoch
9.   Carnoustie Burnside
10. Golspie

STAR RATINGS

★★★★★

Boat of Garten
Carnoustie
Crieff
Cruden Bay
Glasgow Gailes
Gullane
Kingsbarns
Ladybank
Montrose Links Trust

Muirfield
Royal Dornoch
Royal Troon
Southerness
St Andrews Old Golf Course
The Gleneagles Hotel (King's
    Course)
Turnberry Hotel (Ailsa)
Western Gailes

★★★★

Balbirnie Park
Belleisle
Blairgowrie (Rosemount)
Crail
Downfield
Duff House Royal
The Dukes
Dunbar
Edzell
Gullane
Irvine
Kilmarnock
Kingussie
Leven
Loch Lomond
Luffness
Lundin
Machrie Hotel
Machrihanish
Marriott Dalmahoy
Monifieth (Medal)

Moray (Old)
Nairn
North Berwick
Portpatrick
Powfoot
Prestwick
Royal Aberdeen
Royal Musselburgh
Scotscraig
St Andrews (Eden)
St Andrews (Jubilee)
St Andrews (New)
Tain
The Carnegie
The Glen
The Gleneagles Hotel
    (Monarch's Course)
The Gleneagles Hotel (Queen's
    Course)
The Roxburghe

★★★

Aberdour
Alloa

Alyth
Auchterarder

Ballater
Bothwell Castle
Braemar
Brora
Brunston Castle
Bruntsfield Links
Buchanan Castle
Callander
Cardross
Carnoustie Burnside
Cathkin Braes
Cawder
Crow Wood
Deeside
Drumpelier
Duddingston
Dumfries & County
East Renfrewshire
Elgin
Erskine
Forfar
Forres
Fortrose & Rosemarkie
Glasgow
Gleddoch
Glenbervie
Golf House Club
Golspie
Grantown-on-Spey
Green Hotel
Gullane
Haggs Castle
Hawick
Hilton Park
Hopeman
Inverness
Kilmacolm
Kilspindie

King James VI
Kings Acre
Kirkcaldy
Letham Grange
Longniddry
Millport
Moffat
Monifieth (Ashludie)
Moray (New)
Murcar
Murrayshall Hotel
Musselburgh
Nairn Dunbar
Newburgh-on-Ythan
Newmacher (Hawkshill)
Newtonmore
Panmure
Peebles
Pitlochry
Pollock
Portlethen
Prestwick St Cuthbert
Ratho Park
Royal Burgess
Shiskine
Stonehaven
Stranraer
Strathaven
Strathpeffer Spa
Taymouth Castle
Troon Portland
Turnberry Hotel (Arran)
West Linton
West Lothian
Whitekirk Golf Course
Wick
Windyhill

★★

Aboyne
Arbroath Golf Course
Baberton
Ballochmyle

Blairgowrie (Lansdowne)
Braehead
Brechin
Broomieknowie

Camperdown
Carradale
Cathcart Castle
Cochrane Castle
Cowglen
Cullen
Dalmilling
Deer Park
Drumoig
Dullatur
Dunfermline
Elderslie
Fraserburgh
Girvan
Glencruitten
Gourock
Greenburn
Haddington
Hayston
Hazelhead
Huntly
Invergordon
Kemnay
King's Links
Kintore
Kirkhill

Kirriemuir
Lanark
Largs
Lochranza
Lochwinnoch
Loudoun Gowf
Milngavie
Mortonhall
Muir of Ord
Newmacher (Swailend)
Newton Stewart
Paisley
Peterculter
Peterhead
Pitreavie (Dunfermline)
Port Glasgow
Prestonfield
Prestwick St Nicholas
Ralston
Ranfurly Castle
Royal Tarlair
Stirling
Traigh Golf Course
West Kilbride
Westerwood Hotel

★

Braid Hills
Duns
Liberton

Lothianburn
Strathlene
Vale of Leven

Strathclyde

Royal Troon Golf Club ★★★★★

Craigend Road, Troon, KA10 6EP
Nearest main town: Troon

Royal Troon is the centrepiece of a magnificent stretch of courses on the coast of the Firth of Clyde that includes Prestwick and Western Gailes. Unlike, say, Open venues like Muirfield or Turnberry, which are showered with praise by almost all who play there, Troon is a links that suffers from the imbalance of its two halves. They are not that different in length, but the prevailing wind from the south-west makes the back nine very harrowing. On the first day of the 1997 Open Championship, only two players could match the par of 36 on the back nine.

This impression is not helped by the fact that Troon is essentially an out-and-back links, so by the time you step into the teeth of the gale on the 13th, the batteries are already running low. By the time you have reached the 18th, you can feel thoroughly disillusioned with the game and swear never to return to Troon.

Whether you label this a design fault, or merely package it as the slings-and-arrows of playing a championship course, you can't fail to be impressed with some of the holes at Troon. The best holes are at the farthest extreme of the course, starting with the 7th, a sharp dogleg protected by a conical sandhill on the right. They say the next, the Postage Stamp 8th, a par-3 of just 126 yards, is the most difficult stamp in the world to lick, played from an elevated tee into the prevailing wind to a green just 25 feet wide at its widest point. The green is protected by a gully, a sandhill and crater bunkers. The 9th runs round the back of the Postage Stamp, a par-4 of 419 yards where the bunkers on the left protect the best line in – if you're too far right there's no sight of the green, which, unusually, is completely unprotected.

The 10th and 11th are Troon's best two holes. On both occasions, you drive over sand hills to unreceptive, bumpy fairways, from where it's uphill into the wind with a long iron. The 11th, with the railway running just over the stone wall, plays as a par-5 for the members but is one of the most difficult par-4s in the world for the pros.

Troon does not have the dramatic landscapes of other links courses, its definition confined to long wispy grasses and watchtower sandhills. The compensation comes in the form of dramatic views over the Firth of Clyde to the Isle of Arran and the Mull of Kintyre.

Secretary:	Mr J. W. Chandler	Tel: 01292 311555
		Fax: 01292 318204
Professional:	Mr R. B. Anderson	Tel: 01292 313281
		Fax 01292 315977

Playing: Midweek: round £110.00; day n/a. Weekend: round n/a; day n/a. Handicap certificate required.

Facilities: Bar: 11am–11pm. Food: Lunch for visitors on Monday, Tuesday and Thursday only. Includes buffet lunch.

Comments: Visitors Monday, Tuesday & Thursday only. Price includes Old Course round as well ... Have not played it but walked it and reckon the Postage Stamp is one of the best holes in the world ... Overpriced ... Back nine is too tough ... Into the wind on the back nine is toughest experience I've had on any course ... A long, hard slog back ... Best holes are at far end of course ... Best holes from the 9th to the 13th ... Hard to fault ... Still one of the best around ... For the money, not worth it ... Loved it and will be back.

Turnberry Hotel Golf Club (Ailsa)   ★★★★★

Turnberry, KA26 9LT
Nearest main town: Girvan

Turnberry is arguably the most scenically stunning course on the Open Championship rota. The views across to the Isle of Arran and Mull of Kintyre are wondrous, and on a clear day you can sometimes see all the way to Ireland. And looming out of the mid Atlantic swell is the sinister and primeval Ailsa Craig, a 1208ft bulging hunk of rock which lends its name to Turnberry's famous links.

The course, unusually for a links, is run entirely as a commercial operation. There are none of the Rottweiler secretaries you associate with the top private courses, so you should be able to play, although the waiting list is growing. Guests of the first-class hotel, which looms over the course, get preference, so if you really want to treat yourself, book in. If not, you'll just have to wait, but it's worth it.

Turnberry is maintained in absolutely stunning condition. The warts-and-all nature of links golf doesn't seem to apply here, where the fairways rarely get dry and the greens are always holding. It would have been hard to imagine there was a first-class links here in 1945 after the course had been used as an airstrip in the war, a transformation that destroyed many of its natural features. But, under the guidance of Mackenzie Ross, it was revived and stands as a monument to that architect's brilliance.

Turnberry is also blessed with a pleasant micro-climate, the warm air on the Gulf Stream making for pleasant golfing conditions. There are all the perils you associate with Open courses, such as wiry rough, protected greens and sandhills, but it is not particularly wild and many of the tee shots are attractive, from elevated tees to valley fairways. It truly is a very fair test of golf.

For many, the experience of playing Turnberry is purely to stand on the 9th tee, with the waves bludgeoning the rocky outcrop tee, for a drive across cliffs to a camber fairway marked by a stone cairn. But you wouldn't label it Turnberry's best hole. The 16th, a short par-4 called Wee Burn, could lay claim to that; so could any of the eight holes along the coast. The course truly will appeal to all and is the most accessible links for those who prefer the inland game.

Secretary:	Mr E. Bowman	Tel: 01655 331000
		Fax: 01655 331706
Professional:	Mr B. Gunson	Tel: 01655 331000
	(Golf Dir)	Fax 01655 331069
Playing:	Midweek: round £120.00; day n/a. Weekend: round £150.00; day n/a. Handicap certificate required.	
Facilities:	Bar: 11am–11pm. Food: Breakfast, lunch and dinner from 7am–10pm. Bar snacks.	
Comments:	An experience that will live in the memory forever ... Just a wonderful place to play and forget about the world ... Forget the cost, you must play it at least once ... Not to be missed ... Playing the final hole towards the hotel is just a bit special ... Very beautiful ... History, tradition and a superb hotel ... Worth every penny.	

Western Gailes Golf Club

Gailes, Irvine, KA11 5AE
Nearest main town: Troon

Western Gailes will never win any awards for equal opportunities (there are no ladies' tees here), but as a test of golf it is first class. It is not the type of links where the scenery distracts you from your game, neither is there a great deal of variety. The attraction of Western Gailes lies in staying mentally strong enough to combat the ferocious winds that can pick up here. In fact, the second part of the club's name could not be more appropriate.

The course is completely exposed to the winds that race in from the south-west, much like neighbouring Royal Troon. The winds that make the incoming holes at Troon such a contest are the same ones that will send your ball ballooning in the air from the 6th to the 13th at Western Gailes. It is here that you must protect your score before the comparatively easy finishing holes.

The unusual layout of the course, with the clubhouse set in the middle of a narrow piece of tortured, bumpy land, and the holes spreading out in both directions, is intriguing. With the toughest part of the course in the middle, you can completely lose your appetite for the game if things are going badly, and the sorry golfers trudging off the 18th are testament to that. The impression is further confirmed by looking at the faces of the members in the bar, carved completely by the strong winds, and more akin to North Sea cod fishermen than golfers.

One of the club's most distinguished members, Lord Brabazon, once said: 'If you have the time, play just three courses – Western Gailes, Prestwick and Turnberry.' Advice to be taken with a pinch of salt, although you should play Western Gailes.

Secretary: Mr A. M. McBean   Tel: 01294 311649
                                       Fax: 01294 312312

Professional: None.

Playing: Midweek: round £60.00; day £90.00. Weekend: round n/a; day n/a. Handicap certificate required.

Facilities: Bar: 11am–11pm. Food: Lunch and dinner from 11am–10pm.

Comments: Beautifully maintained and managed course ... Excellent facilitites ... What a wonderful traditional course with a warm Scottish welcome ... Warm and friendly clubhouse.

Ballochmyle Golf Club   ★★

Ballochmyle, Mauchline, KA5 6LE
Nearest main town: Mauchline

Secretary: Mr A. Williams   Tel: 01290 550469
                                      Fax: 01290 550469

Professional: None.

Playing: Midweek: round £18.00; day £25.00. Weekend: round n/a; day £30.00. Handicap certificate required.

Facilities: Bar: 11am–11pm. Food: Bar snacks.

Comments: Small greens, plenty of trees … Greens give this course protection against good scoring … Friendly attitude … Will go back for the welcome … Unpretentious club … Course honest, if somewhat unspectacular.

Belleisle Golf Club ★★★★

Belleisle Park, Doonfoot Road, Ayr, KA7 4DU
Nearest main town: Ayr

Secretary:	Mr T. Culter	Tel: 01292 441258
	(Manager)	Fax: 01292 442632
Professional:	Mr D. Gemmell	Tel: 01292 441314
		Fax 01292 441314

Playing: Midweek: round £19.00; day £27.00. Weekend: round £21.00; day £31.00. Handicap certificate required.

Facilities: Bar: 11am–11pm. Food: Breakfast, lunch and dinner from 7am–10pm. Bar snacks.

Comments: One of the best kept and presented public courses … Always in excellent condition – summer or winter … True and fast greens on visit … Tough and pretty.

Bothwell Castle ★★★

Blantyre Road, Bothwell, Glasgow, G81 8PS
Nearest main town: Glasgow

Secretary:	Mr David. McNaught	Tel: 01698 854052
		Fax: 01698 854052
Professional:	Mr Alan. McCloskey	Tel: 01698 852052

Playing: Midweek: round £24.00; day £32.00. Weekend: round n/a; day n/a. Handicap certificate required.

Facilities: Bar: 11am–11pm seasonal. Food: Bar snacks, lunches, high teas, dinners on request. Food at weekends for members.

Comments: Quite short but enjoyable and fun to play ... Basically flat parkland layout – No hills! – but not as open as it used to be because of the 300 trees the club have just planted ... Not difficult to score well on if you are hitting the ball reasonably straight ... Tough finish with a decision to be made about trying to carry the ditch that runs across the fairway at the 510-yard, par-5 16th. Final hole is also a testing 430-yard four played uphill to the green.

Brunston Castle Golf Club   ★★★

Daily, Girvan, KA26 9RH
Nearest main town: Girvan

Secretary:	Mr P. McCloy	Tel: 01465 811471
	(Gen Manager)	Fax: 01465 811545
Professional:	Mr S. Forbes	Tel: 01465 811474

Playing: Midweek: round £26.00; day £40.00. Weekend: round £30.00; day £45.00. Handicap certificate required.

Facilities: Bar: 11am–11pm. Food: Lunch and dinner from 10am–10pm. Bar snacks.

Comments: Nice new course ... Tends to get boggy in wet conditions ... New Donald Steel course ... Praiseworthy design but course can get wet ... Perfect golf facility for novices.

Cardross Golf Club   ★★★

Main Road, Cardross, Dumbarton, G82 5LB
Nearest main town: Dumbarton

Secretary:	Mr Ian T. Waugh	Tel: 01389 841754
		Fax: 01389 842162
	(e-mail cardross@globalnet.co.uk)	
Professional:	Mr Robert Farrell	Tel: 01389 841350

Playing: Midweek: round £25.00; day £35.00. Weekend: No visitors. Handicap certificate required.

Facilities: Bar: 11am–11pm; 1 April – 30 September. Food: 11.30am–3pm Mondays; 11.30am–6pm other days; 21 April – 30 September.

Comments: Inspiring view across the River Clyde from some of the higher vantage points on the course, especially the 2nd and 18th tees ... Mature parkland setting with moderately tight, tree-lined fairways ... Excellent fairways and greens which drain extremely well ... I'm taking a chain saw on my next visit to chop down that lovely tree that sits right in the middle of the 14th fairway! ... Expected the wind to be a bigger factor but the holes are mainly well protected by the trees ...

Carradale Golf Club   ★★

Carradale, PA28 6SA
Nearest main town: Campbeltown

Secretary: Mr E. Graham   Tel: 01583 431335 (Home)
Professional: None.

Playing: Midweek: round n/a; day £8.00. Weekend: round n/a; day £8.00. Handicap certificate required.

Facilities: Bar: None. Food: Hotels next to the course open for catering.

Comments: Nine-holer overlooking the Isle of Arran ... Good views ... So difficult ... Rough terrain and Lilliputian greens – very uncomfortable ... Pay it a visit.

Cathcart Castle Golf Club   ★★

Mearns Road, Clarkston, G76 7YL
Nearest main town: Clarkston

Secretary: Mr I. G. Sutherland   Tel: 0141 638 9449
Professional: Mr S. Duncan   Tel: 0141 638 3436

Playing: Midweek: round £25.00; day £35.00. Weekend: round n/a; day n/a. Handicap certificate required.

Facilities: Bar: 11am–11pm. Food: Lunch and dinner from 10am–9pm. Bar snacks.

Comments: Straightforward course with few tricks ... Mature tree-lined course ... Excellent value for money ... Rather short and unmemorable.

Cathkin Braes Golf Club   ★★★

Cathkin Road, Rutherglen, G73 4SE
Nearest main town: Glasgow

Secretary: Mr H. Millar   Tel: 0141 634 6605
                                       Fax: 0141 634 6605
Professional: Mr S. Bree   Tel: 0141 634 0650
                                       Fax 0141 634 0650

Playing: Midweek: round £25.00; day £35.00. Weekend: round
                 n/a; day n/a. Handicap certificate required.

Facilities: Bar: 11am–11pm. Food: Lunch and dinner from
                 10am–9pm.

Comments: Magnificent course prone to waterlogging and midges
                 ... Wonderful layout but exclusivity should give it a
                 minus rating ... Demanding but expensive ... Absolute
                 luxury ... Fantastic service ... Wonderful course with
                 fantastic scenery ... A dream whether wet or dry ...
                 Moorland treat.

Cawder Golf Club   ★★★

Cadder Road, Bishopbriggs, Glasgow, G64 3QD
Nearest main town: Glasgow

Secretary: Mr Hugh F. Tees   Tel: 0141 772 4180
                                       Fax: 0141 772 4463
Professional: Mr Ken Stevely   Tel: 0141 772 7102

Playing: Midweek: round £30.00; day £35.00. Weekend: round
                 No Visitors; day No Visitors. Handicap certificate
                 required.

Facilities: Bar: 11am–11pm. Food: 11am–11pm.

Comments: Fair challenge but you have to able to hit the ball
                 reasonably well from the tee ... Course gets progres-
                 sively tougher over the back nine – especially the 13th
                 and 16th holes.

Cochrane Castle   ★★

Scott Avenue, Craigstone, Johnstone, PA5 0HF
Nearest main town: Johnstone

Secretary:	J. C. Crown	Tel: 01505 320146
		Fax: 01505 325338
Professional:	J. J. Boyd	Tel: 01505 328465

Playing: Midweek: round n/a; day £17.00. Weekend: round n/a; day £25.00. Handicap certificate required.

Facilities: Bar: None. Food: None.

Comments: One of the toughest opening holes you'll ever play and it's a par-3! ... Nice setting, undulating springy fairways lined with mature trees ... Inspiring view from 4th tee towards Ben Lomond ... Look out for the burn that runs through the course, especially where it passes in front of the green at the par-5 5th ... Good catering and friendly helpful staff.

Cowglen Golf Club ★★

301 Barrhead Road, Glasgow, G46
Nearest main town: Glasgow

Secretary: Mr R. J. G. Jamieson Tel: 01292 266600
Professional: Mr J. McTear   Tel: 0141 649 9401

Playing: Midweek: round £20.00; day n/a. Weekend: round £20.00; day n/a. Handicap certificate required.

Facilities: Bar: 11am-11pm. Food: Lunch and dinner from 10am-10pm.

Comments: There's better around Glasgow ... A club course, not really worth it for visitors ... Views of the Campsie Hills ... You're not missing much if you swerve it.

Crow Wood ★★★

Cumbernauld Road, Muirhead, Glasgow, G69 9JF
Nearest main town: Glasgow

Secretary:	I. McInnes	Tel: 0141 779 4954
		Fax: 0141 779 9148
Professional:	B. Moffat	Tel: 0141 779 1943

Playing: Midweek: round £28.00; day £20.00. Weekend: round n/a; day n/a. Handicap certificate required.

Facilities: Bar: None. Food: None.

Comments: Laid out over the Garnkirk estate this is a well established parkland layout ... Fairways are fairly flat but also
pretty tight ... There are 63 bunkers on the course, so it
might be a good idea to brush up on your sand play
before you pay this course a visit ... Hardest hole on the
course is definitely the par-4 13th ... It's a 453-yard
two-shotter with the approach played to an elevated
green. And if that's not tough enough you also have to
avoid a large oak tree that is positioned in the middle of
the fairway ... Par-3 5th is the strongest of the three short
holes. Plays downhill to a slightly elevated green that has
recently been rebuilt.

Dalmilling Golf Course   ★★

Westwood Avenue, Ayr, KA8 0QY
Nearest main town: Ayr

Secretary: None.
Professional: Mr P. Cheyney   Tel: 01292 263893
                                        Fax 01292 610543

Playing: Midweek: round £13.00; day £20.00. Weekend: round
£14.50; day £26.00. Handicap certificate required.

Facilities: Bar: 11am–8pm. Food: 10am–8pm

Comments: Flat parkland layout but enjoyable to play ... 6th is a
really good short hole; only 120 yds but with water all
round the green ... Greens were a little on the slow side
... Everyone welcoming and friendly.

Drumpelier Golf Club

Drumpelier Avenue, Coatbridge, ML5 1RX
Nearest main town: Coatbridge

Secretary: Mr W. Brownlie   Tel: 01236 428723
Professional: Mr D. Ross   Tel: 01236 432971

Playing: Midweek: round £25.00; day £35.00. Weekend: round
n/a; day No Visiting Groups – Members only. Handicap
certificate required.

Facilities: Bar: 11.30am–midnight. Food: All day – last orders
9.30pm.

Comments: All three short holes have approximately the same yardage but the wind can make a big difference to the length they play ... Scenic parkland layout with the trees only coming into play from a fairly wayward stroke ... Many of the bunkers on the course have been recently upgraded but you won't find them too difficult to escape from ... First and last holes are two of the best on the course. The first is a long par-4, while the 18th is a very strong dog-leg par-4 finishing hole ... Excellent challenge for the low to middle handicapper without being too tough a test for the less experienced player ...

Dullatur Golf Club ★★

Dullatur, Glasgow, G68 OAR
Nearest main town: Cumbernauld

Secretary:	Mrs C. Miller	Tel: 01236 723230
		Fax: 01236 727271
Professional:	Mr D. Sinclair	

Playing: Midweek: round £20.00; day £30.00. Weekend: round £25.00; day £35.00. Handicap certificate required.

Facilities: Bar: 11am–11pm. Food: Lunch and dinner from 10am–9pm.

Comments: Poor holes to get up and down from on lower part of course but otherwise pretty good ... New course designed by Dave Thomas ... Depressing name, depressing course ... Two courses and fair facilities for novices ... Fairly natural new course.

East Renfrewshire Golf Club ★★★

Loganswell, Pilmuir, Newton Mearns, G77 6RT
Nearest main town: Newton Mearns

Secretary:	Mr A. L. Gillespie	Tel: 0141 333 9989
		Fax: 0141 333 9979
Professional:	Mr G. D. Clarke	Tel: 01355 500206

Playing: Midweek: round £30.00; day £40.00. Weekend: round n/a; day n/a. Handicap certificate required.

Facilities: Bar: 11am–11pm. Food: Lunch and dinner from 10am–9pm. Bar snacks.

Comments: Superbly laid out and challenging course ... Very busy ... Holiday course that can get crowded ... Flattish course with plenty of intrigue.

Elderslie Golf Club   ★★

63 Main Road, Elderslie, G77 6RX
Nearest main town: Glasgow

Secretary: Mrs A. Anderson   Tel: 01505 323956
Professional: Mr R. Bowman   Tel: 01505 320032
                                          Fax 01505 320032

Playing: Midweek: round £20.00; day £30.00. Weekend: round n/a; day n/a. Handicap certificate required.

Facilities: Bar: 11am–11pm. Food: Lunch and dinner from 10am–8pm. Bar snacks.

Comments: Fairly easy ... Drop in if you are near Glasgow ... Simple parkland course with little trouble ... Not great value ... Large and welcoming membership.

Erskine Golf Club   ★★★

Bishopton, Paisley, PA7 5PH
Nearest main town: Glasgow

Secretary: Mr T. A. McKillop   Tel: 01505 862302
Professional: Mr P. Thomson   Tel: 01505 862108

Playing: Midweek: round £25.00; day £25.00. Weekend: round Members only; day Members only. Handicap certificate required.

Facilities: Bar: Sunday–Thursday 11am–6pm; Friday 11am–7pm; Saturday 11am–11pm. Food: Sunday–Thursday 11am–5pm; Friday 11am–6.30pm.

Comments: Very visually attractive golf courses with no fewer than eight holes running directly alongside the River Clyde, with the Pentland Hills forming a stunning backdrop ... A course of two halves. First nine is usually the easiest, while the back nine is normally played directly into the prevailing wind ... This is an excellent challenge for the good player, while the fairness of the layout enables the medium to high handicap to also enjoy the course, not to mention the stunning views ... We enjoyed a warm welcome and a memorable day's golf.

Girvan Golf Course ★★

Golf Course Road, Girvan, KA26 9HW
Nearest main town: Ayr – 22 miles to north

Secretary: None.
    Tel: 01465 714272/714346 (Starters)
    Fax: 01465 714346

Professional: None.

Playing: Midweek: round £13.00; day n/a. Weekend: round £16.00; day n/a. Handicap certificate required.

Facilities: Bar: None. Food: None.

Comments: Enjoyable public course features an interesting layout where the opening eight holes play out alongside the beach and the remaining 10 holes are played on parkland terrain ... Pretty short by modern standards but still great fun to play ... Designed by James Braid ... Main hazard on the back nine is the River Girvan, where it comes into play on the 15th hole ... For a comparatively short track it has four of the toughest par-3 holes I've played, with three of the four featured on the course coming into play on the last nine ... Wind off the sea can make the opening holes tough.

Glasgow Gailes Golf Club ★★★★★

Gailes, Irvine, KA11 5AE
Nearest main town: Irvine

Secretary: Mr D. W. Deas
    Tel: 01294 311258
    Fax: 01294 279366

Professional: Mr J. Steven
    Tel: 01294 311561

Playing: Midweek: round £42.00; day £52.00. Weekend: round £47.00; day £47.00. Handicap certificate required.

Facilities: Bar: 11am–11pm. Food: Lunch from 11am–4pm. Bar snacks all day.

Comments: Beguiling course, just heavenly when the sun shines ... Heather-lined course of infinite character ... Ninth-oldest course in the world ... Qualifying course for the Open ... Championship standard links with interesting and varied holes ... A real beauty tucked away on some precious turf ... Always in good order ... Make sure you play it.

Glasgow Golf Club   ★★★

Killermont, Glasgow, G61 2TW
Nearest main town: Glasgow

Secretary: Mr D. W. Deas   Tel: 0141 942 2011
                                       Fax: 0141 942 0770
Professional: Mr J. Steven   Tel: 0141 942 8507

Playing: Midweek: round n/a; day n/a. Weekend: round n/a; day n/a. Handicap certificate required.

Facilities: Bar: Members only. Food: Members only.

Comments: One of the oldest clubs in the world ... Course a little outdated ... Absolutely superb clubhouse ... Wonderful club which also owns Glasgow Gailes ... Very fine park-land course ... Get your driver out here.

Gleddoch Golf Club   ★★★

Langbank, PA14 6YE
Nearest main town: Glasgow

Secretary: Mr D. W. Tierney   Tel: 01475 540304
Professional: Mr K. Campbell   Tel: 01475 540304

Playing: Midweek: round £30.00; day £40.00. Weekend: round £40.00; day £50.00. Handicap certificate required.

Facilities: Bar: 11am–11pm. Food: 11am–11pm.

Comments: Stunning setting overlooking the Clyde Estuary ... Be prepared for a few ups and downs but well worth the effort ... Terrain on some holes can make it almost impossible to keep the ball on the fairway ... The short holes are outstanding ... Clubhouse is pretty small, but the locals were very friendly.

Glencruitten Golf Club   ★★

Glencruitten Road, Oban, PA34 4PU
Nearest main town: Oban

Secretary: Mr A. G. Brown   Tel: 01631 562868
Professional: Mr G. Clark   Tel: 01631 564115

Playing: Midweek: round £16.00; day £16.00. Weekend: round £19.00; day £19.00. Handicap certificate required.

Facilities: Bar: 11am–11pm. Food: Lunch and dinner from 10am–9pm.

Comments: Very short and isolated ... Fun to play ... Don't take it too seriously ... A picture ... Hard walking ... Loads of blind shots.

Gourock Golf Club   ★★

Cowal View, Gourock, PA19 1HD
Nearest main town: Greenock

Secretary: Mr A. D. Taylor   Tel: 01475 631001
                                        Fax: 01475 631001
Professional: Mr G. Coyle   Tel: 01475 636834

Playing: Midweek: round £18.00; day £25.00. Weekend: round £22.00; day £27.00. Handicap certificate required.

Facilities: Bar: 11am–11pm. Food: Lunch from noon–2pm. Dinner from 5pm–7pm.

Comments: Rather hilly moorland track ... Nice facilities at this friendly club ... Views over the Firth of Clyde ... Nothing special for the area.

Haggs Castle Golf Club   ★★★

70 Dumbreck Road, Dumbreck, G41 4SN
Nearest main town: Glasgow

Secretary:	Mr I. Harvey	Tel: 0141 427 1157
		Fax: 0141 427 1157
Professional:	Mr J. McAlister	Tel: 0141 427 3355
		Fax 0141 427 3355

Playing: Midweek: round £27.00; day £38.00. Weekend: round n/a; day n/a. Handicap certificate required.

Facilities: Bar: 11am–11pm. Food: Lunch from 11am–4pm. Dinner by arrangement.

Comments: Mature course which has hosted the Scottish Open ... High, lofted shots needed to elevated greens ... Welcoming private club ... Thoroughly enjoyed it ... Will be back one day ... Well maintained.

Hayston Golf Club   ★★

Campsie Road, Glasgow, G66 1RN
Nearest main town: Glasgow

Secretary:	Mr J. V. Carmichael	Tel: 0141 775 0723
		Fax: 0141 775 0723
Professional:	Mr S. Barnett	Tel: 0141 775 0882

Playing: Midweek: round £20.00; day £30.00. Weekend: round n/a; day n/a. Handicap certificate required.

Facilities: Bar: 11am–11pm. Food: Lunch and dinner from 10am–9pm.

Comments: Very undulating parkland course ... Fair test with good facilities ... By no means a classic but fair to the average player ... Not in great condition.

Hilton Park Golf Club   ★★★

Auldmarroch Estate, Milngavie, G62 7HB
Nearest main town: Glasgow

Secretary:	Mrs J. A. Warnock	Tel: 0141 956 4657
		Fax: 0141 956 4657
Professional:	Mr W. McCondichie	Tel: 0141 956 5125
		Fax 0141 956 5125

Playing: Midweek: round £20.00; day £28.00. Weekend: round n/a; day n/a. Handicap certificate required.

Facilities: Bar: 11am–11pm. Food: Members & guests only.

Comments: Very scenic ... Interesting moorland course with trouble at every turn ... The Hilton far superior to the Allander course ... Good quality course.

Irvine Golf Club ★★★★

Bogside, Irvine, KA12 8SR
Nearest main town: Irvine

Secretary: Mr M. McMann Tel: 01294 275979
Professional: Mr K. Erskine Tel: 01294,275626
  Fax 01294 275626

Playing: Midweek: round £38.00; day £55.00. Weekend: round £55.00; day n/a. Handicap certificate required.

Facilities: Bar: 11am–11pm. Food: Lunch and dinner from 10am–9pm. Bar snacks.

Comments: Very tricky course with good variety of holes ... Excellent variation ... Good welcome ... Interesting parkland course ... Will go again ... Just the ticket for holiday golf.

Kilmacolm Golf Club ★★★

Porterfield Road, Kilmacolm, PA13 4PD
Nearest main town: Paisley

Secretary: Mr D. W. Tinton Tel: 01505 872139
  Fax: 01505 874007
Professional: Mr D. Stewart Tel: 01505 872695

Playing: Midweek: round £20.50; day £30.50. Weekend: round £20.50; day £30.50. Handicap certificate required.

Facilities: Bar: 11am–11pm. Food: Lunch and dinner from noon–9pm. Bar snacks.

Comments: One of the best value smaller courses ... 7th is a bit special ... Moorland course of character.

Kilmarnock Golf Club ★★★★

29 Hillhouse Road, Barassie, Troon, KA10 6SY
Nearest main town: Troon

Secretary: Mr R. L. Bryce   Tel: 01292 313920
                                         Fax: 01292 313920
Professional: Mr G. Howie   Tel: 01292 311322
                                         Fax 01292 311322

Playing: Midweek: round £38.00; day £58.00. Weekend: round
                  n/a; day n/a. Handicap certificate required.

Facilities: Bar: 11am–11pm. Food: Lunch and dinner from
                  11am–9pm. Bar snacks.

Comments: Beautifully presented ... Hard test ... Open qualifying
                  course ... Some blind shots ... A must play in the area
                  ... Better than Troon ... New nine holes a little out of
                  character with the rest ... Sensational seaside links ...
                  Heather-lined fairways and small greens – it's awesome.

Kirkhill Golf Club ★★

Greenlees Road, Glasgow, G72 8YN
Nearest main town: Glasgow

Secretary: Mr J. Sweeney   Tel: 0141 641 3083
                                         Fax: 0141 641 3083
Professional: Mr D. Williamson   Tel: 0141 641 7972
                                         Fax 0141 641 7972

Playing: Midweek: round £20.00; day £25.00. Weekend: round
                  n/a; day n/a. Handicap certificate required.

Facilities: Bar: 11am–11pm. Food: Lunch and dinner from
                  10am–9pm. Bar snacks.

Comments: Designed by the master craftsman, James Braid ... Hard
                  walking ... Need to be fit ... Blasted 1st hole a good
                  indication of what's to come.

Lanark Golf Club

The Moor, Lanark, ML11 7RX
Nearest main town: Glasgow

Secretary: Mr G. H. Cuthill   Tel: 01555 663219
                                          Fax: 01555 663219

Professional: Mr A. White   Tel: 01555 661456

Playing: Midweek: round £24.00; day £36.00. Weekend: round
                  n/a; day n/a. Handicap certificate required.

Facilities: Bar: 11am–11pm. Food: Lunch and dinner from
                  10am–9pm. Bar snacks.

Comments: Difficult-to-read greens made this a struggle ... Superb
                  condition ... Always in good nick and a varied challenge
                  ... A few blind shots ... Short and hilly ... Something
                  different from the norm ... Heathland golf at its best.

Largs Golf Club   ★★

Irvine Road, Largs, KA30 8EU
Nearest main town: Largs

Secretary: Mr D. H. MacGillivray Tel: 01475 673594
                                       Fax: 01475 673594
Professional: Mr R. Collinson   Tel: 01475 686192

Playing: Midweek: round £25.00; day £35.00. Weekend: round
                  £35.00; day £35.00. Handicap certificate required.

Facilities: Bar: 11am–11pm. Food: Lunch and dinner from
                  11am–9pm. Bar snacks.

Comments: Very good club with lovely welcome ... Parkland course
                  of some stature ... Great parkland course with streams
                  affecting several holes ... Good hospitality ... Scotland
                  not known for its parkland golf, but this is an exception
                  ... Homely club ... Made very welcome.

Loch Lomond Golf Club   ★★★★

Rossdhu House, Alexandria, G83 8NT
Nearest main town: Glasgow

Secretary: Mr D. MacDonald   Tel: 01436 655555
                                        Fax: 01436 655550
Professional: Mr C. Campbell   Tel: 01436 655535

Playing: Midweek: round £150.00; day n/a. Weekend: round
                  £150.00; day n/a. Handicap certificate required.

Facilities: Bar: 11am–11pm. Food: Breakfast, lunch and dinner
                  from 7am–10pm. Bar snacks.

Comments: Wonderful layout but very expensive ... Too wet and fragile for extensive playing ... Great practice facilities ... Worth the cost if you get the chance.

Lochranza Golf Club   ★★

Lochranza, Isle of Arran, KA27 8HL
Nearest main town: Brodick

Secretary: Mr I. M. Robertson   Tel: 0177083 0273
                                         Fax: 0177083 0600

Professional: None.

Playing: Midweek: round £12.00; day £16.00. Weekend: round £12.00; day £16.00. Handicap certificate required.

Facilities: Bar: None. Food: None.

Comments: Closed for half the year ... Worth playing if you're going to The Machrie ... Very tough and windy nine-holer on the Isle of Arran ... Great fun.

Lochwinnoch Golf Club   ★★

Burnfoot Road, Lochwinnoch, PA12 4AN
Nearest main town: Paisley

Secretary: Mrs E. Wilson   Tel: 01505 842153
                                         Fax: 01505 843668

Professional: Mr G. Reilly   Tel: 01505 843029

Playing: Midweek: round £15.00; day £20.00. Weekend: round £15.00; day £20.00. Handicap certificate required.

Facilities: Bar: 11am–11pm. Food: Lunch and dinner from 10am–9pm.

Comments: Well kept but not a difficult course ... Useful practice for the high-handicapper ... Rather hilly parkland course.

Loudoun Gowf Golf Club   ★★

Galston, KA4 8PA
Nearest main town: Kilmarnock

Secretary: Mr T. R. Richmond   Tel: 01563 820551
                                         Fax: 01563 822229

Professional: None.

Playing: Midweek: round £18.00; day £30.00. Weekend: round
                   n/a; day n/a. Handicap certificate required.

Facilities: Bar: 11am–11pm. Food: Lunch and dinner from
                   11am–10pm. Bar snacks.

Comments: Very difficult parkland course ... Short but designed to
                   high order ... Nothing you won't find elsewhere ...
                   Worthy of note ... Delightfully named, charming short
                   course.

Machrie Hotel Golf Club   ★★★★

Port Ellen, Isle of Islay, PA42 7AN
Nearest main town: Port Ellen

Secretary: Mr T. Dunn   Tel: 01496 302310
                                           Fax: 01496 302404
Professional: None.

Playing: Midweek: round £20.00; day £30.00. Weekend: round
                   £20.00; day £30.00. Handicap certificate required.

Facilities: Bar: 11am–11pm. Food: Breakfast, lunch and dinner
                   from 7am–10pm. Bar snacks.

Comments: Unique atmosphere and incredibly challenging ...
                   Almost unplayable in really bad weather ... New holes a
                   bit of a let down ... Enjoy the whisky and peat fire in the
                   clubhouse ... Surprising course design but very interest-
                   ing ... Condition excellent ... Incredibly natural course
                   ... Thrilling from start to finish.

Machrihanish Golf Club   ★★★★

Machrihanish, PA28 6PT
Nearest main town: Campbeltown

Secretary: Mrs M. Anderson   Tel: 01586 810213
                                           Fax: 01586 810221
Professional: Mr K. Campbell   Tel: 01586 810277
                                           Fax 01586 810277

Playing: Midweek: round £25.00; day £40.00. Weekend: round
                   £30.00; day £50.00. Handicap certificate required.

Facilities: Bar: 11am–11pm. Food: Breakfast, lunch and dinner
                   from 9am–9pm. Bar snacks.

Comments: Natural setting offering stiff test of golf ... Great links course that is open to the elements ... A wild, windswept course ... Great malt and fantastic people ... Brilliant, and what a nice welcome and people ... A mini Turnberry despite its modest facilities ... Tremendous opening hole to a fantastic links course ... Undulating, wonderful greens ... Cracking opening par-4 over the sea.

Millport Golf Club   ★★★

Millport, Isle of Cumbrae, KA28 OHB
Nearest main town: Millport

Secretary: Mr D. Donnelly   Tel: 01475 530306
                                         Fax: 01475 530306
Professional: Mr K. Docherty   Tel: 01475 530305

Playing: Midweek: round £14.50; day £18.50. Weekend: round £18.50; day £24.50. Handicap certificate required.

Facilities: Bar: 11am–11pm. Food: Lunch and dinner from 10am–9pm. Bar snacks.

Comments: Superb views to Bute, Arran and Kintyre ... Moorland course that can get windy ... Felt very alive here.

Milngavie Golf Club   ★★

Laighpark, Glasgow, G62 8EP
Nearest main town: Glasgow

Secretary: Ms S. McGuinness   Tel: 0141 956 1619
                                         Fax: 0141 956 4252
Professional: None.

Playing: Midweek: round £20.00; day £30.00. Weekend: round n/a; day n/a. Handicap certificate required.

Facilities: Bar: 11am–11pm. Food: Bar snacks. Dinner by arrangement.

Comments: You need to hit the fairways running here ... 1st is a bit special ... Drive over the burn at the 1st is a great way to start ... Scenic course with elements of moorland golf ... Less than 6,000 yards.

Muir of Ord Golf Club   ★★

Great North Road, Muir of Ord, IV6 7SX
Nearest main town: Inverness

Secretary:	Mr D. Noble	Tel: 01463 870825
		Fax: 01463 870825
Professional:	Mr G. Legett	Tel: 01463 871311

Playing: Midweek: round £12.50; day £14.50. Weekend: round £16.50; day £18.50. Handicap certificate required.

Facilities: Bar: 11am–11pm. Food: Bar snacks.

Comments: Very short, eccentric heathland course ... Will test your patience ... Fairways you can stick a cigarette paper between – very tight and suffocating.

Paisley Golf Club   ★★

Braehead, Paisley, PA2 8TZ
Nearest main town: Paisley

Secretary:	Mr M. MacPherson	Tel: 0141 884 3903
		Fax: 0141 884 3903
Professional:	Mr G. Stewart	Tel: 0141 884 4114

Playing: Midweek: round £20.00; day £28.00. Weekend: round £20.00; day £28.00. Handicap certificate required.

Facilities: Bar: 11am–11pm. Food: Lunch and dinner from 10am–9pm. Bar snacks.

Comments: Terrific views and some fine hilly holes ... Good course and interesting greens ... Very windy at times ... Wind the main challenge.

Pollock Golf Club   ★★★

90 Barrhead Road , Glasgow, G43 1BG
Nearest main town: Glasgow

Secretary:	Mr Ian. Cumming	Tel: 0141 632 4351
		Fax: 0141 649 1398
Professional:	None.	

Playing: Midweek: round £32.00; day £42.00. Weekend: round £32.00; day £42.00. Handicap certificate required.

Facilities: Bar: 11am–11pm. Food: Full lunches, snacks, other meals by arrangement.

Comments: Wonderful secluded setting within the grounds of the Pollock Estate ... Great layout with some magnificent mature trees to contend with should you stray too far from the middle of the fairways ... 14th hole is a real challenge where you have to decide just how much of the River Cart you are brave enough to bite off with your tee shot ... Short 6th offers one of the most scenic tee shots on the course ... Nice people who obviously enjoy their golf.

Port Glasgow Golf Club   ★★

Devol Farm, Port Glasgow, PA14 5XE
Nearest main town: Port Glasgow

Secretary: Mr N. L. Mitchell   Tel: 01475 700334
Professional: None.   Tel: 01475 705671

Playing: Midweek: round £15.00; day £20.00. Weekend: round n/a; day n/a. Handicap certificate required.

Facilities: Bar: 11am–11pm. Food: Lunch and dinner from noon–9pm. Bar snacks.

Comments: Views of the Clyde ... Cheap course primarily for beginners ... Short course with basic facilities ... Moorland track open most of the year.

Prestwick Golf Club   ★★★★

2 Links Road, Prestwick, KA9 1QG
Nearest main town: Prestwick

Secretary: Mr I. T. Bunch   Tel: 01292 477404
                                            Fax: 01292 477255
Professional: Mr F. C. Rennie   Tel: 01292 479483

Playing: Midweek: round £65.00; day £90.00. Weekend: round n/a; day n/a. Handicap certificate required.

Facilities: Bar: 11am–11pm. Food: Lunch from 11am–3pm.

Comments: 1st is just so tough, you feel disillusioned before you've got going ... Good fun ... Plenty of blind holes ... History and tradition with terrific holes next to the Firth ... Great value ... So difficult ... Walking in the footsteps of the greats ... An intoxicating experience.

Prestwick St Cuthbert Golf Club ★★★

East Road, Prestwick, KA9 2SX
Nearest main town: Prestwick

Secretary:	Mr J. C. Rutherford

Tel: 01292 477101
Fax: 01292 671730

Professional: None.

Playing: Midweek: round £22.00; day £30.00. Weekend: round n/a; day n/a. Handicap certificate required.

Facilities: Bar: 11am–11pm. Food: Lunch and dinner from 11am–9pm.

Comments: Good test ... Only minus point is flatness of course ... Flat and exposed ... Little attractive to the eye ... Fun on an historic course.

Prestwick St Nicholas Golf Club ★★

Grangemuir Road, Prestwick, KA9 1SN
Nearest main town: Prestwick

Secretary: Mr G. B. S. Thomson Tel: 01292 477608
Fax: 01292 473900

Professional: None.

Playing: Midweek: round £30.00; day £50.00. Weekend: round £35.00; day n/a. Handicap certificate required.

Facilities: Bar: 11am–11pm. Food: Lunch from noon–4pm. Dinner by arrangement.

Comments: Weekend play Sunday only ... Laid out between the sea and the railway line ... A very honest links ... One to savour ... Enormous greens ... Don't leave Prestwick without playing here ... Won't forget it in a hurry.

Ralston Golf Club ★★

Strathmore Avenue, Paisley, PA1 3DT
Nearest main town: Paisley

Secretary: Mr J. Pearson
Tel: 0141 882 1349
Fax: 0141 883 9837

Professional: Mr Colin. Munro
Tel: 0141 810 4925

Playing: Midweek: round £18.00 Visiting parties only; day £28.00 Visiting parties only. Weekend: round No visitors; day No visitors. Handicap certificate required.

Facilities: Bar: Mon–Fri noon–11pm, Sat, Sun 11am–11pm. Food: Kitchen opens at noon – 9.30pm Monday – Friday (coffee and biscuits before noon). Weekends 11am–9.30pm. Bar snacks and Restaurant.

Comments: At least one bunker to avoid on every hole ... Mature parkland but the fairways are tight enough in places to threaten some of the tee shots ... Look our for the ditches that tend to pop up in all the wrong places ... Par-4 2nd which measures 448 yards and plays uphill, is by far the toughest on the course ... Really enjoyed the closing hole. It may measure only 330 yards, but I'm sure the pond that guards the front of the green collects a fair number of golf balls during the season ... Friendly welcome assured ... Clubhouse newly refurbished with good view of 18th hole.

Ranfurly Castle Golf Club   ★★

Golf Road, Bridge of Weir, PA11 3HN
Nearest main town: Paisley

Secretary: Mr J. Walker   Tel: 01505 612609
                                    Fax: 01505 612609
Professional: Mr T. Eckford   Tel: 01505 614795

Playing: Midweek: round £30.00; day £40.00. Weekend: round n/a; day n/a. Handicap certificate required.

Facilities: Bar: 11am–11pm. Food: Lunch and dinner from 10am–9pm. Bar snacks.

Comments: Good Scottish inland golf ... Very challenging and visually attractive ... Not out of the top drawer but good value ... Hard walking ... Tough.

Shiskine Golf Club   ★★★

Shiskine, Isle of Arran, KA27 8HA
Nearest main town: Brodick

Secretary: Mr I. Robertson   Tel: 01770 860226
                                    Fax: 01770 860205
Professional: None.

Playing: Midweek: round £12.00; day £18.00. Weekend: round
                 £15.00; day £20.00. Handicap certificate required.

Facilities: Bar: None. Food: Tea room and snacks all day.

Comments: Wonderful views but course did not match them ...
                 Plenty of blind shots... Could be best value in Britain ...
                 Good greens, great setting and great fun although can
                 get congested ... More boys and girls have learned golf
                 here than at all the private Glasgow and Edinburgh
                 clubs combined ... A gem ... 12 holes only ... Great
                 value ... Great views to Mull of Kintyre ... A pilgrimage
                 to repeat again and again ... You will either love it or
                 hate it.

Strathaven Golf Club ★★★

Glasgow Road, Strathaven, ML10 6NL
Nearest main town: Glasgow

Secretary: Mr A. W. Wallace   Tel: 01357 520421
                                          Fax: 01357 520539
Professional: Mr M. McCrorie   Tel: 01357 521812

Playing: Midweek: round £22.00; day £32.00. Weekend: round
                 n/a; day n/a. Handicap certificate required.

Facilities: Bar: 11am–11pm. Food: Lunch and dinner from
                 10am–9pm.

Comments: Tree-lined course with oodles of character ... One to
                 note ... A respite from the surfeit of links golf in Scotland
                 ... Tight driving and tricky greens ... Always in good
                 condition.

Troon Portland Golf Club ★★★

Troon,
Nearest main town: Troon

Secretary: Mr J. W. Chandler   Tel: 01292 311555
                                          Fax: 01292 318204
Professional: Mr R. Anderson

Playing: Midweek: round n/a; day £35.00. Weekend: round n/a;
                 day £45.00. Handicap certificate required.

Facilities: Bar: 11am–11pm. Food: Lunch and dinner by arrangement. Bar snacks.

Comments: You don't go to Troon to play here ... Enjoyed it but only a warm up to the main challenge ... Good fun.

Turnberry Hotel Golf Club (Arran)   ★★★

Turnberry, KA26 9LT
Nearest main town: Girvan

Secretary: Mr E. Bowman   Tel: 01655 331000
                                 Fax: 01655 331706
Professional: Mr B. Gunson   Tel: 01655 331000
(Golf Dir)   Fax 01655 331069

Playing: Midweek: round £55.00; day n/a. Weekend: round £55.00; day n/a. Handicap certificate required.

Facilities: Bar: 11am–11pm. Food: Breakfast, lunch and dinner from 7am–10pm. Bar snacks.

Comments: Wonderful foil to the Ailsa ... Not easy and sometimes in better condition than the Ailsa ... Top-class second-string course at this luxurious hotel ... Very technical course, very rewarding.

Vale of Leven Golf Club   ★★

Northfield Road, Alexandria, G83 9ET
Nearest main town: Dumbarton

Secretary: Mr J. Stewart   Tel: 01389 752351
Professional: None.

Playing: Midweek: round £18.00; day n/a. Weekend: round £22.00; day n/a. Handicap certificate required.

Facilities: Bar: Noon–11pm. Food: Breakfast, lunch and dinner from 8am–9pm.

Comments: Holes overlook Loch Lomond ... Not in the same league as nearby Loch Lomond ... Very short but unbelievably tricky ... Can get very wet.

West Kilbride Golf Club   ★★

Fullerton Drive, Seamill, West Kilbride, KA23 9HT
Nearest main town: West Kilbride

Secretary: Mr H. Armour   Tel: 01294 823911
                                         Fax: 01294 823911
Professional: Mr G. Ross   Tel: 01294 823042

Playing: Midweek: round n/a; day £37.00. Weekend: round n/a;
                  day n/a. Handicap certificate required.

Facilities: Bar: 11am–11pm. Food: Lunch and dinner from
                  11am–10pm.

Comments: A really strong test off blue tees ... Invariably in great
                  condition ... Warm welcome at a beautiful setting ...
                  Views of the Isle of Arran ... Unheralded but excellent ...
                  Good value compared to a lot of Scottish courses.

Westerwood Hotel Golf & Country Club   ★★

St Andrews Drive, Cumbernauld, G68 1RN
Nearest main town: Glasgow

Secretary: Mr S. Killin   Tel: 01236 452772
                                         Fax: 01236 738478
Professional: Mr S. Killin   Tel: 01236 725281

Playing: Midweek: round £22.50; day £35.00. Weekend: round
                  £27.50; day £45.00. Handicap certificate required.

Facilities: Bar: 11am–11pm. Food: Breakfast, lunch and dinner
                  from 7am–10pm. Bar snacks.

Comments: Need to be long and straight, unlike its designer, Mr
                  Ballesteros ... Will get better ... Imaginative course,
                  what you would expect from Seve ... Beautiful location
                  which course does not live up to ... Ambitious course ...
                  Maybe Seve should stick to his day job.

Windyhill Golf Club   ★★★

Windyhill, Bearsden, G61 4QQ
Nearest main town: Glasgow

Secretary: Mr B. Davidson   Tel: 0141 942 2349
                                         Fax: 0141 942 5874
Professional: Mr G. Collinson   Tel: 0141 942 7157

Playing: Midweek: round n/a; day £20.00. Weekend: round n/a; day n/a. Handicap certificate required.

Facilities: Bar: 11am–11pm. Food: Lunch and dinner from 10am–9pm.

Comments: Not the best near Glasgow but worth a shout ... Nice feel to this open parkland course ... Some good technical holes on the back nine ... Front nine much harder.

Borders and Dumfries & Galloway

Southerness Golf Club ★★★★★

Southerness, Southerness, DG2 8AZ
Nearest main town: Dumfries

When you mention the Solway Firth as an area of natural outstanding golf, Silloth-on-Solway springs immediately to mind. But located almost directly opposite Silloth, across the pond-like calm of the Firth in Scotland, is a course few have heard of. Mention its name, Southerness, and you might still be corrected and told Southerndown, the fine Welsh course. On the map of Britain's golf courses, someone's left a crumb of cake in Southerness.

The course's low profile is possibly because it is something of a rarity, a links course that was only opened in 1947, a second-generation course without the traditional feel and established nature of many of Scotland's great links; it may be because it is not blessed with the same outstanding natural scenery that one expects from a links; or it may be because it was designed by Mackenzie Ross, almost as an afterthought while he was working on the exceptional Ailsa course at Turnberry. Whatever it is, Southerness does not get the credit it deserves.

In design terms it is first-class. There are no blind holes, where you hit your ball and scamper over a dune or hill to see which trap your ball has fallen into. Neither do balls bounce off the fairways after a good drive. Situated on a flat piece of land by the Solway Firth, and covered in gorse, heather and bracken, Southerness is very fair, the scores on each day governed by the wind that rushes in off the sea.

With the character of each hole at the mercy of the wind, Southerness is in a constant flux. One thing that never changes is the quality of the par-4s, particular the 12th, played to a green nesting precariously on the edge of the beach. Neither does the welcome, which is warm and hearty on arrival and in the clubhouse afterwards.

Secretary:	Mr W. D. Ramage	Tel: 01387 880677
		Fax: 01387 880644
Professional:	Mr G. Gray	

Playing: Midweek: round £30.00; day £30.00. Weekend: round £40.00; day £40.00. Handicap certificate required.

Facilities: Bar: 11am–11pm. Food: Lunch and dinner from 11am–9pm. Bar snacks.

Comments: Not a well-known course so invariably in good condition ... Long and windy ... A gem of a course, well worth the visit ... Greens very good ... People just superb.

Dumfries & County Golf Club   ★★★

Nunfield, Edinburgh Road, Dumfries, DG1 1JX
Nearest main town: Dumfries

Secretary: Mr E. C. Pringle   Tel: 01387 253585
Professional: Mr S. Syme   Tel: 01387 268918
                                        Fax 01387 268918

Playing: Midweek: round £23.00; day £23.00. Weekend: round £26.00; day £26.00. Handicap certificate required.

Facilities: Bar: 11am–11pm. Food: Lunch and dinner from 11am–9pm. Bar snacks.

Comments: Runs alongside River Nith ... A long journey to find it but worth the effort ... Parkland beauty sculpted by Willie Fernie ... One of the best examples of Scottish parkland golf ... An unforgettable par-3 14th ... Informative pro shop ... Off the beaten track but good for visitors.

Duns Golf Club   ★★

Hardens Road, Duns, TD11 3NR
Nearest main town: Duns

Secretary: Mr A. Campbell   Tel: 01361 882194
Professional: None.

Playing: Midweek: round £12.00; day £15.00. Weekend: round £15.00; day £20.00. Handicap certificate required.

Facilities: Bar: 11am–11pm. Food: Bar snacks.

Comments: Need to be fit here ... Odd course for an oddly named club ... Burn runs through middle of the course ... Burn dominates the 15th ... A warm welcome guaranteed ... A real Braveheart of a course.

Hawick Golf Club ★★★

Vertish Hill, Hawick, TD9 0NY
Nearest main town: Carlisle – 44 miles, Edinburgh – 52 miles

Secretary: Mr J. Harley   Tel: 01450 372293
Professional: None.

Playing: Midweek: round £20.00; day £25.00. Weekend: round
                  £20.00; day £25.00. Handicap certificate required.

Facilities: Bar: Noon–11pm. Food: Noon–9pm.

Comments: Hilly layout means you have to be fit to really enjoy
                  playing here … Wonderfully peaceful setting, even if
                  some of the holes are a bit of a slog. Great fun to play
                  … Greens a little slow but a great location.

Moffat Golf Club ★★★

Coatshill, Moffat, DG10 9SB
Nearest main town: Beattock

Secretary: Mr T. A. Rankin   Tel: 01683 220020
Professional: None.

Playing: Midweek: round £18.50; day £20.00. Weekend: round
                  £28.00; day £30.00. Handicap certificate required.

Facilities: Bar: 11am–11pm. Food: Bar snacks.

Comments: Take your oxygen tank with you … Up in the gods you
                  certainly need a head for heights … Warm welcome but
                  freezing-cold course … Scenic course overlooking the
                  town.

Newton Stewart Golf Club ★★

Kirroughtree Avenue, Minnigaff, Newton Stewart, DG8 6PF
Nearest main town: Newton Stewart

Secretary: Mr M. Large   Tel: 01671 402172
                                         Fax: 01671 402172
Professional: None.

Playing: Midweek: round £20.00; day £23.00. Weekend: round
                  £23.00; day £27.00.

Facilities: Bar: 11am–11pm Easter until 31 October Friday evenings, Saturday and Sunday. Food: 11am–11pm Easter until 31 October Friday evenings, Saturday and Sunday.

Comments: A true hidden gem ... Ideal place to enjoy golf in a less demanding guise ... Spray the ball about and you can easily run up a bunch of bogies ... Plenty of room from the tee ... Greens receptive all year ... Five very individual par-3s a speciality ... Visitors welcome ... Buggies available ... Pre-booking suggested in summer ... Golf/food packages available.

Peebles Golf Club   ★★★

Kirkland Street, Peebles, EH45 8EO
Nearest main town: 23 miles due south of Edinburgh

Secretary: Mr H. T. Gilmore   Tel: 01721 720099
Professional: Mr C. Imlah   Tel: 01721 720197

Playing: Midweek: round £20.00; day £27.00. Weekend: round £25.00; day £34.00. Handicap certificate required.

Facilities: Bar: 11am–11pm summer. Food: All day up to 9pm.

Comments: Not too demanding but design always presents different challenges ... Tough opening two holes, the 200-yard par-3 1st is followed by an equally demanding par-4 2nd ... Flattering, provided you can keep the ball straight ... Short 16th is the best hole on the course ... Very attractive setting and friendly staff.

Portpatrick Golf Club   ★★★★

Golf Course Road, Portpatrick, DG9 8TB
Nearest main town: Stranraer

Secretary: Mr J. A. Horberry   Tel: 01776 810273
                                       Fax: 01776 810811
Professional: None.

Playing: Midweek: round £18.00; day £27.00. Weekend: round £21.00; day £32.00. Handicap certificate required.

Facilities: Bar: 11am–11pm. Food: Lunch and dinner from 11am–9pm. Bar snacks.

Comments: Remote links with bundles of character ... Course defence entirely dictated by the wind ... Wonderfully old-fashioned links ... Will linger in the memory for a long time ... Village simply breathes golf ... Very exposed.

Powfoot Golf Club   ★★★★

Cummertrees, Annan, DG12 5QE
Nearest main town: Annan

Secretary: Mr B. W. Sutherland   Tel: 01461 700276
                    (Manager)   Fax: 01461 700276
Professional: Mr G. Dick   Tel: 01461 700327
                                           Fax 01461 700327

Playing: Midweek: round £23.00; day £30.00. Weekend: round £23.00; day £30.00. Handicap certificate required.

Facilities: Bar: 11am–11pm. Food: Lunch and dinner from 11am–9pm. Bar snacks.

Comments: Superb condition and nice surroundings ... A classic links ... Good layout, difficult in the wind.

The Roxburghe Golf Course   ★★★★

Sunlaws House Hotel, Kelso, TD5 8JZ
Nearest main town: Kelso

Secretary: Mr D. MacIntyre   Tel: 01573 450331
Professional: Mr G. Niven   Tel: 01573 450333
                                           Fax 01573 450611

Playing: Midweek: round £35.00; day n/a. Weekend: round £60.00; day n/a. Handicap certificate required.

Facilities: Bar: 11am–11pm. Food: Breakfast, lunch and dinner from 9am–9pm. Bar snacks.

Comments: Excellent new course ... The 5th and 6th are exceptional holes ... Shop and food a little pricey ... When fully mature this will be a bit special ... Was allowed to use championship tees so a great welcome ... Anyone know a better new course? ... Best new course in Scotland since Loch Lomond.

Stranraer Golf Club ★★★

Creachmore, Stranraer, DG9 0LF
Nearest main town: Stranraer

Secretary:　　Mr Bryce C. Kelly　　　Tel: 01776 870245
　　　　　　　　　　　　　　　　　　Fax: 01776 870445

Professional: None.

Playing:　　Midweek: round £20.00; day £29.00. Weekend: round £25.00; day £35.00. Handicap certificate required.

Facilities:　　Bar: 11am–11pm. Food: Snacks, bar meals and full meals.

Comments:　　One of the best courses in the Southwest of Scotland ... Great scenery, especially the views towards Loch Ryan ... Good test of golf, especially when the wind blows ... New clubhouse is a big improvement ... Another cracker by James Braid.

Fife and Clackmannan

Kingsbarns Golf Club ★★★★★

Kiingsbarns Links, Kingsbarns, St Andrews, KI6 8QD
Nearest main town: St Andrews

'This is one of the last true seaside links capable of development in
Scotland. It is a wonderful course and, though man-made, it has a
totally natural feel. I have no doubt the course has championship potential.' Those are the words of Sir Michael Bonallack, former Secretary of
the R&A and now the Captain of the world-famous club.

Now, Sir Michael knows a thing or two about what it takes to make
a great championship golf course. Therefore when he speaks in such
glowing terms, especially about a newly-built course, the golfing world
really has to sit up and take notice.

The stunning new links course at Kingsbarns is situated some eight
miles south of St Andrews, along a mile and a half of magnificent coastline overlooking the North Sea. Part of this spectacular site takes in an
old nine-hole course dating back to 1793, which was taken over by the
military in 1938 but never opened again after the end of the Second
World War.

The rest of the land consisted of two large areas of fairly flat farm-
land, which have been superbly sculpted to create a course destined to
become one of the best built in Britain over the past 100 years.
Kingsbarns is laid out on two distinctly different levels, and the outstanding design has taken full advantage of this dramatic change in elevation
to create a layout providing truly spectacular views of the sea from all
18 holes.

This is a golf course littered with great holes. However, the 185-
yard par-3 15th, played across a rocky bay to a slender green
surrounded on three sides by the sea, is among the best and certain
to become one of the most photographed holes in golf. Likewise the
556-yard par-5 12th, which follows the broad sweep of the shoreline,
will ruin more than a few scorecards on days when the wind whips
in from the North Sea. Finally, the 445-yard par-4 18th, normally
played into the prevailing wind, provides the type of challenging
finishing hole you would expect to find of a potential championship
course.

Secretary: To be appointed.   Tel: 01334 880222 Bookings
                                     Fax: 880496
Professional: Mr D. Scott

Playing: Midweek: round £85.00 Visitors; day £85.00 Visitors.
Weekend: round £85.00 Visitors; day £85.00 Visitors.
Handicap certificate required.

Facilities: Bar: Full facilities from mid-July 2000. Food: Full facilities from mid-July 2000.

Comments: Stunning design ... Newly built but definitely destined to become one of the best links courses not just in Scotland but anywhere in the world ... Superb views of the sea from every single hole on the course ... When the wind blows you will hit every club in the bag ... Looks so natural I can't believe it hasn't been here for over 100 years ... Finishing stretch of holes is just fantastic ... Great variety of classic links holes and a layout every golfer from pro to rabbit will enjoy playing.

Ladybank Golf Club   ★★★★★

Annsmuir, Ladybank, KY15 7RA
Nearest main town: Cupar

Ladybank is, unquestionably, one of the great inland courses of Scotland. While Gleneagles is often rated the premier inland course, on account of the combined grace and splendour of its clubhouse and course, Ladybank is sold purely on the strength of its heathland charm. Situated in the heart of Fife, it is a picturesque course with a profusion of heather, wiry broom and pine trees. It's a course you'll want to play at least once.

The course was originally laid out by Tom Morris in 1879 and has gradually been extended. But the new holes that were added are in keeping with the original design, and there's an agreed game-plan for the player to adhere to – namely accuracy. Ladybank is not a course where you blithely whip the driver out of the bag on the tee, but rather one where the view from the tee consistently argues with you to take an iron. This makes it a very long course at over 6,600 yards, but with usually only one safe way in to the green it is a prudent policy.

Of course, the technical aspects of the game are not what everyone comes to Ladybank for; rather they come to marvel at the pines, heather and gorse, which give the course a sublime feel and smell. In many respects it resembles the famed Surrey heath and heather courses, but unlike them there's also thick swathes of wild grasses and secondary rough of an almost brush-wire character, which clings to the hosel of your club.

The best hole on the course is probably the 16th, a sharp dogleg to the left where there is only one real line – down the middle – followed by an approach shot to a left-to-right sloping green with trees on the left. It's indicative of many holes at Ladybank, a visual and technical puzzle that you leave feeling as though you've only scratched the surface.

Secretary: Mr I. F. Sproule   Tel: 01337 830814
                                              Fax: 01337 831505
Professional: Mr M. J. Gray   Tel: 01337 830725

Playing: Midweek: round £28.00; day £40.00. Weekend: round £35.00; day n/a. Handicap certificate required.

Facilities: Bar: 11am–11pm. Food: Lunch and dinner from 10am–9pm. Bar snacks.

Comments: Excellent test of golf in beautiful surroundings ... Well prepared ... Good all-round test ... Gorse is the main hazard here ... Excellent practice facilities ... Best time to play is in the autumn ... Very nice experience – warm clubhouse and course in top nick ... Forget about St Andrews, this is the best in Fife ... A golfer's golf course ... Tough but rewarding ... Set in exquisite mature woodland ... Pine trees, heather and gorse – perfect ... Really is the business ... Preferred it to all the Open courses ... Very easy on the eye.

St Andrews Old Golf Course   ★★★★★

St Andrews Links Trust, St Andrews, KY16 9SF
Nearest main town: St Andrews

No more than a flat, vast open playing field. Made redundant by the improvements in golf club technology. These are just two of the criticisms levelled at the Old Course at St Andrews, the home of the Royal and Ancient Golf Club and the most famous golf course in the world. It has almost become fashionable to have a pop at the Old Course – once, they say, a venerable work of art, but its colours are now fading and its brush strokes are criticised for their broadness and depth.

It wasn't always like this. The bunkers were once praised for their depth and singularity, the double greens for their design and surreal appearance, the double fairways for their uniqueness. But opinions change, and as the game of golf grows and players seek out virgin territory, so the memories of the Old Course fade. Why the stark barrenness of the Old Course when you can have the deep colours and exhilaration of a County Down or a Turnberry?

What the Old Course will do is make you think. If the design is such a joke, why is it so difficult? Huge greens and wide fairways are normally associated with good scoring, and yet, with the exception of the pros, who can make a mockery of the front nine at times, you'll struggle to better your handicap. The answer lies in the illusions the landscape offers. From the tee you are presented with huge fairways, but you see only rutted, unreceptive ones. For your approaches, you are presented with huge greens, but they are often blind and so contoured that your ball runs off in all directions. Then there's the fickle wind, which can grab your ball in mid-flight and deposit it in a scrape or burn.

The Old Course will also make you nervous. First-tee nerves for golfers are as normal as the common cold, but you'll never have experienced anything like this — and the irony is that the fairway you'll be aiming at is the biggest anywhere in the world. Then there's the 17th, a hole so difficult you'll treat it like walking on egg shells and leave with an eight. That's the difficulty at St Andrews. Much like meeting your favourite celebrity, you'll clam up and the right words won't come out.

Secretary: Mr A. J. R. McGregor Tel: 01334 466666
(General Manager)   Fax: 01334 477036

Professional: None.

Playing: Midweek: round £75.00; day n/a. Weekend: round £75.00; day n/a. Handicap certificate required.

Facilities: Bar: 11am–11pm. Food: Breakfast, lunch and dinner from 7am–9pm.

Comments: Sheer magic ... Anyone who's ever professed to be a golfer must play ... Take a caddie ... So subtle ... Feel the nerves on the 1st tee ... The course and the people, the best anywhere ... Tee shot at the 1st is so special ... Take away the 1st, 17th and 18th and this is a very ordinary links ... Course not up to much but the special feeling makes up for it ... It can be both cruel and kind ... A wonderful and mystical venue — not to be missed ... Treasure the experience.

Aberdour Golf Club   ★★★

Seaside Place, Aberdour, Aberdour, KT3 OTX
Nearest main town: Dunfermline

Secretary:	Mr T. H. McIntyre	Tel: 01383 860080
		Fax: 01383 860050
Professional:	Mr G. McCallum	Tel: 01383 860256
		Fax 01383 860256

Playing: Midweek: round £17.00; day £28.00. Weekend: round £17.00; day £28.00. Handicap certificate required.

Facilities: Bar: 11am–11pm. Food: Lunch and dinner from 11am–9pm. Bar snacks.

Comments: Short course on nice piece of coastline ... Good views ... Great wee seaside course with lovely views.

Alloa Golf Club   ★★★

Schawpark, Sauchie, Alloa, FK10 3AX
Nearest main town: Alloa

Secretary:	Mr T. Crampton	Tel: 01259 722745
Professional:	Mr W. Bennett	Tel: 01259 724476
		Fax 01259 724476

Playing: Midweek: round £20.00; day £30.00. Weekend: round £25.00; day £35.00. Handicap certificate required.

Facilities: Bar: 11am–11pm. Food: Lunch and dinner from 11am–9pm. Bar snacks.

Comments: Hilly course with plenty of blind shots ... Strategic bunkering with sunken greens ... Nice stop-over in otherwise barren golfing region ... Worth seeking out ... Reasonable green fees.

Balbirnie Park Golf Club   ★★★★

Balbirnie Park, Markinch, Glenrothes, KY7 6NR
Nearest main town: Glenrothes

Secretary:	Mr S. Oliver	Tel: 01592 612095
		Fax: 01592 612383
Professional:	Mr D. F. G. Scott	Tel: 01592 752006
		Fax 01592 752006

Playing: Midweek: round £25.00; day £33.00. Weekend: round £30.00; day £40.00. Handicap certificate required.

Facilities: Bar: 11am–11pm. Food: Lunch and dinner from noon–9pm. Bar snacks.

Comments: One of the best parkland courses around with a high degree of difficulty ... Still quite young but great fairways, and greens will improve ... Excellent and unusual club ... Compact links with views of Isle of Man on a clear day.

Crail Golfing Society   ★★★★

Balcomie Clubhouse, Fifeness, Crail, KY10 3XN
Nearest main town: St Andrews

Secretary:	Mr J. F. Horsfield	Tel: 01333 450686
		Fax: 01333 450416
Professional:	Mr G. Lennie	Tel: 01333 450960
		Fax 01333 450960

Playing: Midweek: round £22.00; day £35.00. Weekend: round £27.00; day £45.00. Handicap certificate required.

Facilities: Bar: 11am–11pm. Food: Breakfast, lunch and dinner from 7am–10pm. Bar snacks.

Comments: Beautiful part of the world ... Course in excellent nick ... Best holes by the sea ... Very friendly ... One of the oldest clubs in the world ... Superb little links ... Very hospitable ... Friendly Scottish links of the highest quality ... Greens true and fast ... Good holiday golf.

Drumoig Golf Hotel   ★★

Drumoig, Leuchars, St Andrews, KY16 0BE
Nearest main town: Dundee

Secretary:	Mr Douglas Sievwright	Tel: 01382 541800
Professional:	None.	

Playing: Midweek: round £25.00; day n/a. Weekend: round £30.00; day n/a. Handicap certificate required.

Facilities: Bar: 11am–11pm. Food: noon–9.30pm.

Comments: A long slog on the back tees ... Still fairly new but maturing nicely ... Water comes into play in the shape of two large ponds that guard the 5th and 13th greens. Undulating layout but pretty open with generous landing areas from most of the tees ... Drumoig also plays host to The Scottish Golf Centre, which boasts the most advanced and comprehensive practice and teaching centre in Europe ... Some interesting holes especially the ones where the layout incorporates some of the old quarries that were on the original site ... 7,000 yards from the back tees.

The Dukes Golf Course ★★★★

Old Course Hotel Golf Resort & Spa, St Andrews, KY16 9NSP
Nearest main town: St Andrews

Secretary: Mr S. Toon   Tel: 01334 479947
                                Fax: 01334 479456

Professional: Mr J. Kelly

Playing: Midweek: round £50.00; day n/a. Weekend: round £55.00; day n/a. Handicap certificate required.

Facilities: Bar: 11am–11pm. Food: Breakfast, lunch and dinner from 7am–10pm. Bar snacks.

Comments: Quality course ... Panoramic views over the old town ... Can be extremely difficult when the wind blows ... Can tear your game apart ... If you like to be humbled, go here ... Harder than the Old Course ... Who said St Andrews was just about the Old Course?

Dunfermline Golf Club ★★

Pitfirrane, Crossford, Dunfermline, KY12 8QW
Nearest main town: Dunfermline

Secretary: Mr R. De Rose   Tel: 01383 723534
Professional: Mr S. Craig   Tel: 01383 729061

Playing: Midweek: round £20.00; day £30.00. Weekend: round £25.00; day £35.00. Handicap certificate required.

Facilities: Bar: 11am–11pm. Food: Lunch and dinner from 11am–9pm. Bar snacks.

Comments: Weekend play on Sundays only ... Nice parkland course
                   ... Have fun ... Course has stood the test of time ...
                   Rough and semi-rough too punishing on visitors ...
                   Internal out-of-bounds very frustrating.

Glenbervie Golf Club   ★★★

Stirling Road , Larbert, FK5 4SJ
Nearest main town: Falkirk

Secretary: Dr Sheila E. Hartley   Tel: 01324 562605
                                            Fax: 01324 551054
Professional: Mr John. Chillas   Tel: 01324 562725

Playing: Midweek: round £30.00; day £40.00. Weekend: round
                   n/a; day Members' Guests only. Handicap certificate
                   required.

Facilities: Bar: 11am–11pm summer. Food: 10.30am–8pm
                   summer.

Comments: Mature parkland layout ... Look out for the ditch that
                   comes into play on a number of holes ... Super condi-
                   tion with excellent greens and fairways ... You will die
                   happy if you manage to par the 407-yard par-4 14th ...
                   The short 4th is a beauty ... Moderate number of
                   bunkers and not too tight or too long for the average
                   golfer ... James Braid design.

Golf House Club   ★★★

Elie, Leven, KY9 1AS
Nearest main town: St Andrews

Secretary: Mr A. Sneddon   Tel: 01333 330301
                                            Fax: 01333 330895
Professional: Mr R. Wilson   Tel: 01333 330955
                                            Fax 01333 330955

Playing: Midweek: round £32.00; day £45.00. Weekend: round
                   £40.00; day £55.00. Handicap certificate required.

Facilities: Bar: 11am–11pm. Food: Breakfast, lunch and dinner
                   from 9am–9pm. Bar snacks.

Comments: With 16 par-4s and two par-3s this course is full of quirks ... Excellent holiday golf here ... James Braid grew up here ... Located virtually in the middle of the village ... Bump-and-run is a shot you need ... Eccentric course with numerous semi-blind shots.

Kirkcaldy Golf Club   ★★★

Balwearie Road, Kirkcaldy, KY2 5LT
Nearest main town: Kirkcaldy

Secretary: Mr A. C. Thomson   Tel: 01592 205240
                                    Fax: 01592 205240
Professional: Mr A. Caira   Tel: 01592 203258
                (Director of Golf)

Playing: Midweek: round £16.00; day £22.00. Weekend: round £22.00; day £32.00. Handicap certificate required.

Facilities: Bar: 11am–11pm. Food: Lunch and dinner from noon–9pm. Bar snacks.

Comments: Challenging parkland course ... Nicely kept, simple course that is surprisingly challenging ... In play most of the year.

Leven Links   ★★★★

The Promenade, Leven, KY8 4HS
Nearest main town: Leven

Secretary: Mr S. Herd   Tel: 01333 421390
                                    Fax: 01333 428859
Professional: None.

Playing: Midweek: round £25.00; day £35.00. Weekend: round £30.00; day £40.00. Handicap certificate required.

Facilities: Bar: 11am–11pm. Food: Breakfast, lunch and dinner from 8am–9pm. Bar snacks.

Comments: Short course but wind stiffens things up ... Right next to Lundin ... Pure links ... Finishes with a flourish ... Real appreciation of the game at this club ... Has stood the test of time ... Always beautifully prepared.

Lundin Golf Club   ★★★★

Golf Road, Lundin Links, KY8 6BA
Nearest main town: Leven

Secretary: Mr D. R. Thomson   Tel: 01333 320202
                                         Fax: 01333 329743
Professional: Mr D. K. Webster   Tel: 01333 320051

Playing: Midweek: round £28.00; day £36.00. Weekend: round
                  £36.00; day n/a. Handicap certificate required.

Facilities: Bar: 11am–11pm. Food: Lunch and dinner from
                  10am–9pm. Bar snacks.

Comments: Weekend play on Saturday afternoons only ... Very hard
                  and interesting course ... Greens are exceptional, while
                  fairways can be scrappy ... Superb welcome ... Unusual
                  course with challenging tee shots ... A parkland/links
                  hybrid that's fun to play ... Old railway runs through the
                  middle ... Let creativity be your watchword.

Pitreavie (Dunfermline) Golf Club   ★★

Queensferry Road, Dunfermline, KY11 8PR
Nearest main town: Dunfermline

Secretary: Mr Eddie Comerford   Tel: 01383 822591
                                         Fax: 01383 722591
Professional: Mr Colin Mitchell   Tel: 01383 723151
                                         Fax 01383 723151

Playing: Midweek: round £26.00; day n/a. Weekend: round
                  £38.00; day n/a. Handicap certificate required.

Facilities: Bar: 11am–11pm. Food: All day.

Comments: Fun course, but not as easy as you might think when you
                  consider it plays just over 6,000 yards ... Well main-
                  tained. Friendly welcome ... Surprised to discover the
                  course was designed by Dr Alistair McKenzie, the man
                  who also created Augusta National ... Little gem.

Scotscraig Golf Club   ★★★★

Golf Road, Tayport, DD6 9DZ
Nearest main town: St Andrews

Secretary: Mr K. Gourlay   Tel: 01382 552515
                                          Fax: 01382 553130
Professional: Mr S. J. Campbell   Tel: 01382 552855

Playing: Midweek: round £27.00; day £36.00. Weekend: round
                   £32.00; day £44.00. Handicap certificate required.

Facilities: Bar: 11am–11pm. Food: Lunch and dinner from
                   10am–9pm. Bar snacks.

Comments: Almost as hard as Carnoustie but without the hype ...
                   Deep bunkers on this links/heathland track ... Enjoyed it
                   immensely ... Lives up to its brutal reputation ... Greens
                   hard to read.

St Andrews Eden Golf Course   ★★★★

St Andrews Links Trust, St Andrews, KY16 9SF
Nearest main town: St Andrews

Secretary: Mr A. J. R. McGregor Tel: 01334 466666
                                         Fax: 01334 477036
Professional: None.

Playing: Midweek: round £23.00; day n/a. Weekend: round
                   £23.00; day n/a. Handicap certificate required.

Facilities: Bar: 11am–11pm. Food: Breakfast, lunch and dinner
                   from 7am–9pm.

Comments: Excellent condition of greens ... The flair of St Andrews
                   also very nice ... A great course for winter golf ... Play
                   it every year ... Much more fun than other St Andrews
                   courses ... Outstanding group of par-3s ... Played it in
                   a sea mist – excellent!

St Andrews Jubilee Golf Course   ★★★★

St Andrews Links Trust, St Andrews, KY16 9SF
Nearest main town: St Andrews

Secretary: Mr A. J. R. McGregor Tel: 01334 466666
                   (General Manager)   Fax: 01334 477036
Professional: None.

Playing: Midweek: round £35.00; day n/a. Weekend: round
                   £35.00; day n/a. Handicap certificate required.

Facilities: Bar: 11am–11pm. Food: Breakfast, lunch and dinner from 7am–9pm.

Comments: Tough cookie when the wind blows...From the back tees this can be a real challenge ... Longest course at St Andrews ... Requires deep reserves of concentration ... The toughest of all the St Andrews courses ... Found it so tough in the wind ... Lacks a bit of atmosphere ... Hard in the wind.

St Andrews New Golf Course   ★★★★

St Andrews Links Trust, St Andrews, KY16 9SF
Nearest main town: St Andrews

Secretary: Mr A. J. R. McGregor Tel: 01334 466666
(General Manager)   Fax: 01334 477036
Professional: None.

Playing: Midweek: round £35.00; day n/a. Weekend: round £35.00; day n/a. Handicap certificate required.

Facilities: Bar: 11am–11pm. Food: Breakfast, lunch and dinner from 7am–9pm.

Comments: Better than the Old Course with some very strong holes ... Similar demands to the Old Course ... Preferred it to the Old ... Great experience but too expensive ... Surprisingly undulating – soak up the atmosphere and prepare for the Old Course.

Lothian

Muirfield Golf Club ★★★★★

Gullane, Gullane, EH31 2EG
Nearest main town: Edinburgh

If you have managed to arrange a game at Muirfield, what you score on the course is largely of secondary importance. This is, after all, the course where, in 1998, US Open champion Payne Stewart – so tragically killed in a plane crash the following year – could not get on after being told it was a members' day. Stewart played instead at Gullane, from where the views of Muirfield suggested it was almost empty.

Protocol has become more relaxed since those days. The club, the Honourable Company of Edinburgh Golfers, is more open to approaches from players wishing to play the course, for years considered the best course in Britain and Ireland.

Muirfield is an astonishing links. It consists of nine holes arranged in a circular shape around the boundaries of the club, with the back nine forming the inner circle. There are no dunes as such, just yawning bunkers, thick rough and 18 subtly contoured greens. One of Muirfield's outstanding features is its turf, which is very fine and tends to dry out quickly as it lies on top of pure sand. This can give the course a different character from day to day: on the Saturday, an American-style target-golf course, and on the Sunday, a typical links.

You get an early indication of what is to come at the 1st, a 449-yard par-4, where the pitfalls of missing the fairway will become immediately apparent. By the time you come off the par-3 4th, you will be doing better than average if you've yet to land in one of the bunkers, which seem to be depositaries for balls which land short of the green.

An unusual split-level fairway, situated on a dogleg, defines the 6th, before the final three holes on the front nine that will make or break your score. The 8th is probably the toughest of the trio, where 12 bunkers guard the right-hand side of the fairway, forcing you to the left and giving you a longer approach shot.

The back nine is not as tough as, say, a Troon or a Carnoustie, with birdie chances at the 14th, 15th and 17th, but it finishes with a bang, a devilish par-4 18th that is a fitting climax. Jack Nicklaus once described Muirfield as the fairest Open course he knew, and there is no greater praise than that.

Secretary: Mr J. A. Prideaux   Tel: 01620 842123
                                       Fax: 01620 842977
Professional: None.

Playing: Midweek: round £70.00; day £95.00. Weekend: round
                 n/a; day n/a. Handicap certificate required.

Facilities: Bar: 11am–11pm. Food: Lunch from noon–2pm.

Comments: Visitors on Tuesday & Thursday only ... The best course
                 I have ever played which is what it is all about ... A bit
                 of a mystery why it is voted No. 1 in the rankings ...
                 Sadly, strange rules if you want to play ... Died and gone
                 to heaven ... Just heaven ... True sense of history ...
                 Thick rough, deep bunkering.

Baberton Golf Club   ★★

50 Baberton Avenue, Juniper Green , Edinburgh, EH14 5DU
Nearest main town: Edinburgh

Secretary: Mr Alan G. Boe (Acting) Tel: 0131 453 4911
Professional: Mr Ken Kelly   Tel: 0131 453 3555

Playing: Midweek: round £20.00; day £30.00. Weekend: round
                 n/a; day n/a. Handicap certificate required.

Facilities: Bar: 11am–11pm. Food: available.

Comments: Well established parkland layout ... Scenic views
                 towards Edinburgh, some five miles away ... Some of
                 the toughest par-3s you will find anywhere ... 16th is the
                 toughest par-4. All uphill, 467 yards into the wind ...
                 Staff and members very sociable and friendly.

Braid Hills Golf Club   ★★

Braid Hills Road, Edinburgh, EH10 6JY
Nearest main town: Edinburgh

Secretary: None.   Tel: 0131 447 6666
Professional: None.

Playing: Midweek: round £8.50; day n/a. Weekend: round
                 £8.50; day n/a. Handicap certificate required.

Facilities: Bar: None. Food: None.

Comments: One of the best public courses in the UK. ... Tough, challenging with tight fairways and gorse ... Fun to play.

Broomieknowie Golf Club Limited ★★

36 Golf Course Road, Bonnyrigg, EH19 2HZ
Nearest main town: Dalkeith

Secretary: Mr J. G. White   Tel: 0131 663 9317
                                     Fax: 0131 663 2152
Professional: Mr Mark. Patchett   Tel: 0131 660 2035

Playing: Midweek: round £17.00; day £25.00. Weekend: round £20.00; day n/a. Handicap certificate required.

Facilities: Bar: In season – all day. Food: Food is available

Comments: Established parkland layout with some climbs between the holes, but otherwise fairly flat ... Toughest hole is the dogleg par-4 7th. Enjoyed the short par-3 5th which drops down some 50 feet from the tee and offers a nice view to the south ... Good general condition ... Newly refurbished clubhouse provides good value food all day during the summer.

Bruntsfield Links Golfing Society ★★★

The Clubhouse, 32 Barnton Avenue, Edinburgh, EH4 6JH
Nearest main town: Edinburgh

Secretary: Cdr D. M. Sandford   Tel: 0131 336 2006
                                     Fax: 0131 336 5538
Professional: Mr B. Mackenzie   Tel: 0131 336 4050

Playing: Midweek: round £36.00; day £50.00. Weekend: round £42.00; day £55.00. Handicap certificate required.

Facilities: Bar: 11am–11pm. Food: Lunch from 12.30pm–2.30pm.

Comments: Magnificent parkland ... Heavenly scenery ... Good course and best lunch to be had in Edinburgh ... Excellent restaurant ... Food better than the course.

Deer Park CC ★★

Knightsbridge, Livingston, EH54 9PG
Nearest main town: Edinburgh

Secretary:	I. Thomson	Tel: 01506 431037
		Fax: 01506 435608
Professional:	W. Yule	

Playing: Midweek: round £16; day £22. Weekend: round £26; day £32. Handicap certificate required.

Facilities: Bar: n/a. Food: n/a.

Comments: First nine fairly flat but you will have to be pretty fit to tackle the back nine which is more up and down ... Par-5 15th a real tester played uphill all the way. But the climb is worth making because the view from the top to Edinburgh and the Forth Bridge is stunning ... Superb off-course facilities which include – believe it or not – 16 ten-pin bowling alleys ... Par-3 10th makes an excellent start to the back nine.

Duddingston Golf Club

Duddington Road West, Edinburgh, EH15 3QD
Nearest main town: Edinburgh

Secretary:	Mr M. Corsa	Tel: 0131 661 7688
	(Manager)	Fax: 0131 661 4301
Professional:	Mr A. Mclean	Tel: 0131 661 4301

Playing: Midweek: round £27.00; day £36.00. Weekend: round £27.00; day £36.00. Handicap certificate required.

Facilities: Bar: 11am–11pm. Food: Lunch from noon–2pm. Dinner by arrangement.

Comments: The most welcoming and challenging of the parkland courses around Edinburgh – underrated ... Braid's Burn the main hazard ... A course designed for the average player ... Sporting track very near centre of Edinburgh.

Dunbar Golf Club

East Links, Dunbar, EH42 1LT
Nearest main town: Dunbar

Secretary:	Mrs L. Thom	Tel: 01368 862317
		Fax: 01368 865202
Professional:	Mr D. Small	Tel: 01368 862086
		Fax 01368 862086

Playing: Midweek: round £25.00; day £35.00. Weekend: round £35.00; day £45.00. Handicap certificate required.

Facilities: Bar: 11am–11pm. Food: Lunch and dinner from 10am–9pm.

Comments: Singular links character ... A cracking links and a great test in the wind ... Great hospitality and value ... Excellent links with tight fairways and slap-you-on-the-back welcome ... Classic East Lothian links ... Bracing ... On a rocky outcrop, this is marvellous ... Wind races around this links ... A lonely experience on a cold day ... Best holes around the turn.

Greenburn Golf Course   ★★

6 Greenburn Road, Fauldhouse, Edinburgh, EH47 9HG
Nearest main town: Edinburgh

| Secretary: | Mr J. Irvine | Tel: 01506 635309 |
| Professional: | Mr M. Leighton | Tel: 01501 771187 |

Playing: Midweek: round on application; day on application. Weekend: round on application; day on application. Handicap certificate required.

Facilities: Bar: None. Food: None.

Comments: Very pleasant moorland layout. The location is fairly high up but the course itself is comparatively flat in nature ... Easy walking course and ideal if you are the type of golfer who is keen to play two rounds in the one day ... Not a great deal of trouble to contend with and the fairways are reasonably wide ... Layout quite open but well bunkered ... Four shot holes with the best being the 6th, which plays around 160 yards with a stream guarding the back of the green and bunkers in front ... Pick of the par-4 holes is the 18th, only 350 yards, but out of bounds all the way down the left side, bunkers on the right and trees around the green making the second shot difficult if your tee shot finishes in the wrong place!

Gullane Golf Club (No. 1)   ★★★★★

Gullane, Gullane, EH31 2BB
Nearest main town: Edinburgh

Secretary:	Mr S. C. Owram	Tel: 01620 842255
		Fax: 01620 842327
Professional:	Mr J. Hume	Tel: 01620 843111

Playing: Midweek: round £54.00; day £80.00. Weekend: round £67.00; day n/a. Handicap certificate required.

Facilities: Bar: 11am–11pm. Food: Lunch from noon–2.30pm except Monday–Wednesday.

Comments: Beautiful links course ... Excellent greens ... Bunkers are almost unfair ... Vastly underrated ... Greens as fast as anything played ... Great greens and view ... Wonderful greens and a windy course ... Austere-looking course ... Basic course but golf as it should be played ... Don't bother with No. 2 or No. 3, this is the one ... You can see Muirfield from the highest point here.

Gullane Golf Club (No. 2)   ★★★★

Gullane, Gullane, EH31 2BB
Nearest main town: Edinburgh

Secretary:	Mr S. C. Owram	Tel: 01620 842255
		Fax: 01620 842327
Professional:	Mr J. Hume	Tel: 01620 843111

Playing: Midweek: round £14.00; day £21.00. Weekend: round £18.00; day £26.00. Handicap certificate required.

Facilities: Bar: 11am–11pm. Food: Lunch from noon–2.30pm except Monday–Wednesday.

Comments: Very well presented and managed – businesslike approach ... Fair welcome from helpful staff ... Comfortable, modern clubhouse ... Excellent short links to play with friends.

Gullane Golf Club (No. 3)   ★★★

Gullane, Gullane, EH31 2BB
Nearest main town: Edinburgh

Secretary:	Mr S. C. Owram	Tel: 01620 842255
		Fax: 01620 842327
Professional:	Mr J. Hume	Tel: 01620 843111

Playing: Midweek: round £23.00; day £35.00. Weekend: round £29.00; day £44.00. Handicap certificate required.

Facilities: Bar: 11am–11pm. Food: Lunch from noon–2.30pm except Monday-Wednesday.

Comments: Clearly the second best links at Gullane ... Fairly open ... Not far behind No. 1 ... Lives in the shadow of No. 1.

Haddington Golf Club ★★

Amisfield Park, Haddington, EH41 4PT
Nearest main town: Haddington

Secretary:	Mr Stuart Wilson	Tel: 01620 823627
		Fax: 01620 826580
Professional:	Mr John Sandilands	Tel: 01620 822727

Playing: Midweek: round £18.00; day £26.00. Weekend: round £23.00; day £32.00. Handicap certificate required.

Facilities: Bar: 10.30am–11pm summer (or dusk). Food: All day March/October.

Comments: Parkland course laid out in the grounds of an old country house ... Interesting – if rather flat ... Look out for additional water hazards currently being constructed ... The par-4 15th is a card-wrecker with water running all the way down the left side ... The uphill par-3 8th is played virtually blind ... Clubhouse could be improved.

Kilspindie Golf Club ★★★

Aberlady, Longniddry, EH32 0QD
Nearest main town: Aberlady

Secretary:	Mr R. M. McInnes	Tel: 01875 870358
		Fax: 01875 870358
Professional:	Mr G. J. Sked	Tel: 01875 870695

Playing: Midweek: round £20.00; day £30.00. Weekend: round £25.00; day £35.00. Handicap certificate required.

Facilities: Bar: 11am–11pm. Food: Lunch from 10am–3pm.

Comments: Old course which has been overtaken by technology ...
Short and tight ... Old links with superb bunkering ...
Natural test of any golfer ... 8th is a stunner ...
Everything links golf should be ... A little short ... Step
back in time.

Kings Acre Golf Club   ★★★

Lasswade, Edinburgh, EH18 1AW
Nearest main town: Edinburgh

Secretary: Mrs Elizabeth King   Tel: 0131 663 3456
                                         Fax: 0131 663 7076
Professional: Mr Alan Murdoch   Tel: 0131 663 3456
                                         Fax 0131 663 7076

Playing: Midweek: round £15.00; day n/a. Weekend: round
£21.00; day n/a. Handicap certificate required.

Facilities: Bar: 11am–11pm. Food: 9am onwards.

Comments: New layout but superb design ... Watch out for the water
... First nine fairly open but then the layout gets a bit
tighter on the homeward run ... Greens in great nick
considering how young the course is ... If you make par
at the 13th you can go home a happy golfer ... Excellent
clubhouse and facilities ... Great value for money.

Liberton Golf Club   ★★

297 Gilmerton Road, Edinburgh, EH16 5UJ
Nearest main town: Edinburgh

Secretary: Mrs B. Giefer   Tel: 0131 664 3009
                                         Fax: 0131 664 0853
Professional: Mr I. Seath   Tel: 0131 6641056
                                         Fax 0131 6581988

Playing: Midweek: round £17.00; day £30.00. Weekend: round
£30.00; day n/a. Handicap certificate required.

Facilities: Bar: 11am–11pm. Food: Lunch and dinner from
11am–10pm. Bar snacks.

Comments: A bit of everything at this short parkland course ... A little
easy ... Nice routeing ... Wooded in places.

Musselburgh Golf Club ★★★

Monktonhall, Musselburgh, EH21 6SA
Nearest main town: Musselburgh

Secretary: Mr E. Stoddart   Tel: 0131 665 2005
Professional: Mr F. Mann   Tel: 0131 665 7055
                                        Fax 0131 665 7055

Playing: Midweek: round £18.00; day £25.00. Weekend: round £21.00; day £30.00. Handicap certificate required.

Facilities: Bar: 11am–11pm. Food: Lunch and dinner from 10am–8pm. Bar snacks.

Comments: Really interesting course ... Not overly challenging until the 18th ... Course right next to an oil production plant ... The view has to be seen to be believed.

North Berwick Golf Club ★★★★

West Links, Beach Road, North Berwick, EH39 4BB
Nearest main town: North Berwick

Secretary: Mr A. G. Flood   Tel: 01620 895040
                                        Fax: 01620 893274
Professional: Mr D. Huish   Tel: 01620 893233

Playing: Midweek: round £36.00; day £54.00. Weekend: round £54.00; day £70.00. Handicap certificate required.

Facilities: Bar: 11am–11pm. Food: Lunch and dinner from 10am–10pm. Bar snacks.

Comments: Attractive, welcoming course ... Real links golf with roads, walls, burns, humps and hollows ... Knee-length rough a bit of a bind ... A course with everything ... Really fun course – what the game is all about ... The ideal place to be, not as busy as Gullane and twice as welcoming ... Great location and best course in the area ... Designed by the sands of time ... Watch out for the famous Redan ... Prepare to be humbled by the North Berwick experience ... We would die for something like this in the States.

Prestonfield Golf Club   ★★

6 Priestfield Road North, Edinburgh, EH16 5HS
Nearest main town: Edinburgh

Secretary: Mr A. S. Robertson   Tel: 0131 667 9665
                                          Fax: 0131 667 9665
Professional: Mr J. MacFarlane   Tel: 0131 667 8597
                                          Fax 0131 667 9665

Playing: Midweek: round £20.00; day £30.00. Weekend: round
                  £30.00; day £40.00. Handicap certificate required.

Facilities: Bar: 11am–11pm. Food: All day.

Comments: Pleasant parkland layout that is not too tight from the
                  tee... Some great panormaic views, especially from the
                  first tee, which looks directly towards Arthur's Seat in
                  Edinburgh ... Par-4 4th is probably the toughest hole on
                  the course, especially if you tangle with the trees ...
                  Decent off-course facilities.

Ratho Park Golf Club   ★★★

Ratho, Newbridge, EH28 8NX
Nearest main town: Edinburgh

Secretary: Mr J. Yates   Tel: 0131 333 1752
                                          Fax: 0131 333 1752
Professional: Mr Allan. Pate   Tel: 0131 333 1406

Playing: Midweek: round £25.00; day £35.00. Weekend: round
                  £35.00; day n/a. Handicap certificate required.

Facilities: Bar: 11am–11pm   seasonal.   Food: 11am–
                  4pm and 6pm–9pm, Monday limited catering – soup
                  and toasties.

Comments: Comparatively flat course that is easy on the legs ...
                  Attractive layout runs through the Ratho Park estate with
                  lots of flowers in bloom around the course during the
                  summer months ... Didn't find the fairways all that wide
                  at times , but they were never tight enough to make me
                  feel really inhibited ... Pleasant, if not all that challeng-
                  ing ... The clubhouse is a beautiful 19th-century
                  building ... Especially enjoyed the short 15th. Measuring
                  161 yards and played downhill to a green that is almost
                  completely surrounded with bunkers, it's not surprising
                  to discover that the hole is named 'Sandy Hollow.'

Royal Burgess Golfing Society of Edinburgh   ★★★

181 Whitehouse Road, Barnton, Edinburgh, EH4 6BY
Nearest main town: Edinburgh

Secretary: Mr J. P. Audis   Tel: 0131 339 2075
                                       Fax: 0131 339 3712
Professional: Mr G. Yuille   Tel: 0131 339 6474
                                       Fax 0131 339 6474

Playing: Midweek: round £37.00; day £47.00. Weekend: round
                  n/a; day n/a. Handicap certificate required.

Facilities: Bar: 11am–11pm. Food: Bar snacks.

Comments: Highly conditioned ... Fairways like greens at some
                  clubs ... Magnificent ... Accuracy more important than
                  distance ... Historic course with many nice features ...
                  Greens superb.

Royal Musselburgh Golf Club   ★★★★

Prestongrange House, Prestonpans, EH32 9RP
Nearest main town: Edinburgh

Secretary: Mr T. H. Hardie   Tel: 01875 810276
                                       Fax: 01875 810276
Professional: Mr J. Henderson   Tel: 01875 810139
                                       Fax 01875 810139

Playing: Midweek: round £20.00; day £35.00. Weekend: round
                  £35.00; day n/a. Handicap certificate required.

Facilities: Bar: 11am–11pm. Food: Lunch from 10am–4pm.
                  Dinner by arrangement.

Comments: Rather unbalanced with just one par-5 ... Special feel to
                  this venerable parkland layout ... Spirit in which golf
                  should be played ... Very strategic bunkering ... Usually
                  can be found in fine condition.

The Glen Golf Club   ★★★★

East Links, North Berwick, EH39 4LE
Nearest main town: North Berwick

Secretary: Mr D. R. Montgomery Tel: 01620 895288
                                       Fax: 01620 895447

Professional: None.   Tel: 01620 894596

Playing: Midweek: round £17.00; day £26.00. Weekend: round
                 £22.00; day £30.00. Handicap certificate required.

Facilities: Bar: 11am–11pm. Food: Lunch and dinner from
                 10am–8pm.

Comments: Good old-fashioned golf club with no over-the-top
                 features ... The East Links of North Berwick ... Views
                 over the Firth of Forth ... Blind shots all over the place
                 ... Highlight was the 18th, left me with great impression
                 of the course.

West Linton Golf Club   ★★★

Medwyn Road, West Linton, Edinburgh, EH46 7HN
Nearest main town: Edinburgh

Secretary: Mr Alex J. Mitchell   Tel: 01968 660970
                                         Fax: 01968 660970
Professional: Mr Ian Wright   Tel: 01968 660256

Playing: Midweek: round £20.00; day £30.00. Weekend: round
                 £30.00; day n/a. Handicap certificate required.

Facilities: Bar: 11am–11pm. Food: All day – weekends,
                 11am–9pm – weekdays, summertime.

Comments: Located around 1,000 feet above sea level the course
                 offers some stunning views of the surrounding country-
                 side ... Wind is nearly always a factor ... The layout may
                 measure just over 6,000 yards, but it usually plays every
                 inch of that ... Lovely moorland layout ... Excellent
                 condition ... One of the toughest closing holes in golf
                 and it's a par-3!

West Lothian Golf Club   ★★★

Airngath Hill, Linlithgow, Edinburgh, EH49 7RH
Nearest main town: Edinburgh

Secretary: Mr M. J. Todd   Tel: 01506 825060
                                        Fax: 01506 826030
Professional: Mr N. Robertson   Tel: 01506 825060

Playing: Midweek: round on application; day on application.
                 Weekend: round on application; day on application.
                 Handicap certificate required.

Facilities: Bar: 11am–11pm. Food: Breakfast, lunch and dinner from 7am–10pm. Bar snacks.

Comments: So many cherished memories ... Finest links anywhere ... Golf as it should be ... Magical Northern gem ... Course and facilities excellent ... Good test of golf and good facilities ... Only drawback is remoteness, but still worth the journey ... It's not a frightening course but it can put egg on your face quite easily ... Very hard but fair course ... Just about worth the price of the trip ... A magical, classical links of charm and beauty ... A natural beauty ... Donald Ross country ... Miles from anywhere, a haven of tranquillity ... The best experience in 40 years of golf ... A real tear jerker.

Boat of Garten Golf Club ★★★★★

Boat of Garten, PH24 3BQ
Nearest main town: Inverness

Secretary: Mr P. Smyth Tel: 01479 831282
Fax: 01479 831523
Professional: Mr J. R. Ingram Tel: 01479 831282

Playing: Midweek: round £21.00; day £26.00. Weekend: round £26.00; day £31.00. Handicap certificate required.

Facilities: Bar: 11am–11pm. Food: Breakfast, lunch and dinner from 9.30am–8pm. Bar snacks.

Comments: Good food, not to be missed ... Magnificent surroundings ... How golf should be played ... Maybe overrated ... An unfair course in the summer when the ball bounces everywhere ... Great location – I want to die here ... They get everything right here ... Superb scenery, absolutely compelling golf ... A little too hilly in places to be considered a great ... Had a great day.

Brora Golf Club ★★★

Golf Road, Brora, KW9 6QS
Nearest main town: Dornoch

Secretary: Mr J. Fraser Tel: 01408 621417
Fax: 01408 622157
Professional: None.

Playing: Midweek: round £20.00; day £25.00. Weekend: round £20.00; day £25.00. Handicap certificate required.

Facilities: Bar: 11am–11pm. Food: Lunch and dinner from noon–9pm.

Comments: Excellent hospitality ... Nice links course with good holes ... Electric fences rather annoying ... Friendly sheep on the fairways ... Perfect hospitality ... Any weaknesses the course has are made up for in the 19th ... An experience ... Elevated tees.

The Carnegie Club ★★★★

Skibo Castle, Clashmore, Dornoch, IV25 3RQ
Nearest main town: Dornoch

Secretary: Mr C. Oak　　　　Tel: 01862 894600
　　　　　　　　　　　　　　Fax: 01862 894601
Professional: Mr G. Finleyson　Tel: 01862 881260

Playing: Midweek: round £130.00; day n/a. Weekend: round n/a; day n/a. Handicap certificate required.

Facilities: Bar: 11am–11pm. Food: Lunch from 12.30pm–3pm.

Comments: Some tight holes near Dornoch Firth, but excellent for a new course ... Not worth the cost but undoubted brilliance ... Gulped at the price and course.

Elgin Golf Club ★★★

Hardhillock, Birnie Road, Elgin, IV30 3SX
Nearest main town: Elgin

Secretary: Mr D. F. Black　　　Tel: 01343 542338
　　　　　　　　　　　　　　Fax: 01343 542341
Professional: Mr I. Rodger　　Tel: 01343 542884
　　　　　　　　　　　　　　Fax 01343 542884

Playing: Midweek: round £22.00; day £29.00. Weekend: round £28.00; day £35.00. Handicap certificate required.

Facilities: Bar: 11am–11pm. Food: Lunch and dinner from 10am–9pm. Bar snacks.

Comments: Good course, useful driving range ... Pro shop is consistently helpful to visitors ... Short but don't be fooled ... One of the best inland courses in Scotland ... In the top three parkland courses in Scotland ... A nice change from the surfeit of links.

Forres Golf Club   ★★★

Muiryshade, Forres, IV36 0RD
Nearest main town: Forres

Secretary: Mrs M. Greenaway   Tel: 01309 672949
                                        Fax: 01309
Professional: Mr S. Aird   Tel: 01309 672250
                                        Fax 01309 672250

Playing: Midweek: round £18.00; day £25.00. Weekend: round £20.00; day £27.00. Handicap certificate required.

Facilities: Bar: 11am–11pm. Food: Lunch and dinner from 10am–9pm. Bar snacks.

Comments: People at club could not do enough for the visitors ... Very up and down but nicely run club with good reception ... Well drained ... Welcoming visitors course.

Fortrose & Rosemarkie Golf Club   ★★★

Ness Road East, Fortrose, IV10 8SE
Nearest main town: Inverness

Secretary: Mrs M. Collier   Tel: 01381 620529
                                        Fax: 01381 620529
Professional: None.

Playing: Midweek: round £17.00; day £25.00. Weekend: round £23.00; day £30.00. Handicap certificate required.

Facilities: Bar: 11am–11pm. Food: Lunch from noon–2pm. Dinner by arrangement.

Comments: Tight and tricky, but excellent ... Good place to play and absorb the game ... Sited on Black Isle ... Brute force the main weapon here ... Value for money ... Sea often in play ... Tough nut to crack.

Golspie Golf Club ★★★

Ferry Road, Golspie, KW10 6ST
Nearest main town: Dornoch

Secretary: Mrs M. MacLeod   Tel: 01408 633266
                                          Fax: 01408 633393
Professional: None.

Playing: Midweek: round £18.00; day £20.00. Weekend: round
                  £18.00; day £25.00. Handicap certificate required.

Facilities: Bar: 11am–11pm. Food: Lunch from noon–3pm. Dinner
                  by arrangement.

Comments: Part links, part heathland ... Good variety of golf in
                  pretty surroundings ... The only course with six seaside
                  holes, six heathland holes and six inland holes ... Well
                  kept and visitors made very welcome ... Far from the
                  crowds ... A must in conjunction with Brora and Royal
                  Dornoch.

Grantown-on-Spey Golf Club ★★★

Golf Course Road, Grantown-on-Spey, PH26 3HY
Nearest main town: Aviemore

Secretary: Mr J. A. Matheson   Tel: 01479 872079
                                          Fax: 01479 873725
Professional: Mr B. Mitchell   Tel: 01479 872398

Playing: Midweek: round n/a; day £18.00. Weekend: round n/a;
                  day £23.00. Handicap certificate required.

Facilities: Bar: 11am–11pm. Food: Lunch and dinner from
                  11am–9pm. Bar snacks.

Comments: Play it along with Boat of Garten ... Enjoy the air up here
                  ... Wonderfully fresh and exhilarating course ... A little
                  easy but the scenery is just perfect ... A treasured location
                  near the rambling centre of Aviemore ... Completely
                  unknown so excellent value ... Who said short courses
                  were boring? ... Very eccentric but had a ball.

Hopeman Golf Club ★★★

Hopeman, Moray, IV30 2YA
Nearest main town: Elgin

Secretary: Mr R. Johnston   Tel: 01343 830578
                                       Fax: 01343 830152
Professional: None.

Playing: Midweek: round £15.00; day £20.00. Weekend: round
                  £20.00; day £25.00. Handicap certificate required.

Facilities: Bar: 11am–11pm. Food: Lunch and dinner from
                  10am–3pm. Dinner by arrangement.

Comments: Cracking course ... The 12th one of the best par-3s in
                  all of golf ... Links near the Moray Firth ... You hit and
                  hope at the 12th ... Par-3 is so memorable ...
                  Unbelievable value for classic links experience.

Invergordon Golf Club   ★★

King George Street, Invergordon, IV18 0BD
Nearest main town: Invergordon

Secretary: None.   Tel: 01349 852715
Professional: None.

Playing: Midweek: round £15.00; day £20.00. Weekend: round
                  £15.00; day £20.00. Handicap certificate required.

Facilities: Bar: Full Bar. Food: Bar meals.

Comments: The 11 new holes blend in nicely with the rest of the
                  course ... Fairly flat but scenic setting ... Enjoyed the 9th
                  with the huge rhododendron bushes around the tee ...
                  Watch out for the out of bounds all the way along the
                  railway line on the right side of the 17th and 18th holes
                  ... Very friendly welcome.

Inverness Golf Club   ★★★

Culcabock Road, Inverness, IV2 3XQ
Nearest main town: Inverness

Secretary: Mr G. Thomson   Tel: 01463 239882
                                       Fax: 01463 239882
Professional: Mr A. P. Thomson   Tel: 01463 231989

Playing: Midweek: round £25.00; day n/a. Weekend: round
                  £30.00; day n/a. Handicap certificate required.

Facilities: Bar: 11am–11pm. Food: Lunch from noon–3pm. Dinner
                  by arrangement.

Comments: Flattish with very little definition ... A little overpriced for what you get ... Enjoyed myself thoroughly at this perfect little venue ... Parkland track in prime golfing country.

Kingussie Golf Club ★★★★

Gynack Road, Kingussie, PH21 1LR
Nearest main town: Kingussie

Secretary: Mr N. D. MacWilliam Tel: 01540 661600
Fax: 01540 662066

Professional: None.

Playing: Midweek: round £15.00; day £18.00. Weekend: round £17.00; day £22.00. Handicap certificate required.

Facilities: Bar: 11am–11pm. Food: Breakfast, lunch and dinner from 10am–8pm.

Comments: Short but has all the shots and wonderful greens ... Highlands course up in the sky ... Very soft fairways ... Course plays longer than length ... Epitome of golfing in Scotland – scenic and good welcome ... Good value but could do with a practice ground.

Moray Golf Club (Old) ★★★★

Stotfield Road, Lossiemouth, IV31 6QS
Nearest main town: Elgin

Secretary: Mr B. Russell   Tel: 01343 812018
Fax: 01343 815102

Professional: Mr A. Thomson   Tel: 01343 813330
Fax 01343 813330

Playing: Midweek: round £30.00; day £40.00. Weekend: round £40.00; day £50.00. Handicap certificate required.

Facilities: Bar: 11am–11pm. Food: Breakfast, lunch and dinner from 9am–9pm. Bar snacks.

Comments: Finishing hole is a cracker ... Unknown links ... Starts and ends in the town ... Views over the Moray Firth.

Moray Golf Club (New) ★★★

Stotfield Road, Lossiemouth, IV31 6QS
Nearest main town: Elgin

Secretary:	Mr B. Russell	Tel: 01343 812018
		Fax: 01343 815102
Professional:	Mr A. Thomson	Tel: 01343 813330

Playing: Midweek: round £17.00; day £22.00. Weekend: round £25.00; day £30.00. Handicap certificate required.

Facilities: Bar: 11am–11pm. Food: Breakfast, lunch and dinner from 9am–9pm. Bar snacks.

Comments: Designed by Henry Cotton ... Does not have the same special feel as the Old ... Very favourable climate for good golf ... Not a patch on the Old.

Nairn Dunbar Golf Club ★★★

Lochloy Road, Nairn, IV12 5AE
Nearest main town: Nairn

Secretary:	Mr J. Scott-Falconer	Tel: 01667 452741
		Fax: 01667 456897
Professional:	Mr B. R. Mason	Tel: 01667 453964

Playing: Midweek: round £25.00; day £33.00. Weekend: round £30.00; day £40.00. Handicap certificate required.

Facilities: Bar: 11am–11pm. Food: Breakfast, lunch and dinner from 7am–9pm.

Comments: Hard slog but technically good ... Three new holes are poor and badly out of character ... Good new clubhouse but the other Nairn has Scotland's best new clubhouse ... 10th hole the best ... Unattractive course devoid of a links feel.

Nairn Golf Club ★★★★

Seabank Road, Nairn, IV12 4HB
Nearest main town: Nairn

Secretary:	Mr J. Somerville	Tel: 01667 453208
		Fax: 01667 456328
Professional:	Mr R. Fyfe	Tel: 01667 452787
		Fax 01667 451315

Playing: Midweek: round £50.00; day n/a. Weekend: round £50.00; day n/a. Handicap certificate required.

Facilities: Bar: 11am–11pm. Food: Lunch and dinner from 10am–9pm. Bar snacks.

Comments: Course was a bit disappointing and not worth the trip ... Joy to play ... Long way north but well worth the trip ... Memorable challenge you want to repeat again and again ... Very reasonable course ... Wonderful course presentation and greens ... Outstanding new clubhouse ... A little expensive but well worth the treat ... One of the truly great Scottish links ... Greens quick ... Silky, fast greens ... Devoid of natural beauty but tough as old boots ... Don't forget to take your game with you ... Bunkering and greens exceptional.

Newtonmore Golf Club   ★★★

Golf Course Road, Newtonmore, PH20 1AT
Nearest main town: Inverness 45 miles, Aviemore 15 miles

Secretary: Mr G. Spinks   Tel: 01540 673873
Professional: Mr R. Henderson PGA.   Tel: 01540 673611

Playing: Midweek: round £15.00; day £18.00. Weekend: round £17.00; day £23.00. Handicap certificate required.

Facilities: Bar: 11am–11pm. Food: Full catering except Thursday

Comments: Super setting alongside the River Spey ... Not long but long enough! ... Tremendous value ... Very friendly club ... Setting too nice to worry about how I was scoring ... Everyone was so helpful and friendly.

Strathpeffer Spa   ★★★

Golf Course Road, Strathpeffer, IV14 9AS
Nearest main town: Dingwall

Secretary: Mr N. Roxburgh   Tel: 01997 421396
Professional: No Pro/Club Administrator
                  Mrs Hazel. Slater   Tel: 01997 421011
                                         Fax 01997 421011

Playing: Midweek: round £14.00; day £20.00. Weekend: round £14.00; day £20.00. Handicap certificate required.

Facilities: Bar: 11am–midnight (11.30pm Sunday). Food: During bar hours; package (food and golf) available.

Comments: Basically flat but wonderfully scenic ... Loved the firm springy turn on the fairways, 5th has to be one of the very best short holes on the planet ... Has an almost heathland look and feel ... Great value if you play midweek ... Pleasant clubhouse and reasonable facilities.

Tain Golf Club   ★★★★

Tain, IV19 1PA
Nearest main town: Dornoch

Secretary: Mrs K. D. Ross   Tel: 01862 892314
                                          Fax: 01862 892099

Professional: None.

Playing: Midweek: round £21.00; day £27.00. Weekend: round £25.00; day £31.00. Handicap certificate required.

Facilities: Bar: 11am–11pm. Food: Lunch from 10am–3pm. Dinner by arrangement.

Comments: Dornoch is the top course in the area but you must visit this one too ... Heather and links, a great combination ... Exceptional value ... Very unfashionable course ... Playing here is like a chess match ... Have a clear game plan.

Traigh Golf Course   ★★

Traigh, Arisaig, PH39 4NT
Nearest main town: Fort William

Secretary: Mr W. Henderson   Tel: 01687 450645
Professional: None.   Fax: 01687 450337

Playing: Midweek: round £12.00; day £12.00. Weekend: round £12.00; day £12.00. Handicap certificate required.

Facilities: Bar: n/a. Food: n/a.

Comments: Marvellous evocative course with vistas to the islands of Rhum and Skye ... Only nine holes but don't let that put you off ... A couple of memorable holes ... Views make up for what course so noticeably lacks.

Wick Golf Club   ★★★

Reiss, Wick, KW1 4RW
Nearest main town: Wick

Secretary: Mr D. Shearer   Tel: 01955 602935
Professional: None.

Playing: Midweek: round n/a; day £15.00. Weekend: round n/a;
                    day £15.00. Handicap certificate required.

Facilities: Bar: None. Food: Bar snacks. Lunch and dinner by
                    arrangement.

Comments: Not worth the trek ... Northernmost course in the British
                    Isles ... Very rugged and a little unfair in places ...
                    Wonderful people here ... Course a little eccentric.

Angus and Perth & Kinross

Carnoustie Golf Club ★★★★★

Links Parade, Carnoustie, DD7 7JE
Nearest main town: Dundee

When the Open Championship finally returned to Carnoustie in 1999 after an absence of 24 years, this long and at times brutal links course, which was once called the 'Sleeping Giant', certainly lived up to its reputation as one of the toughest, if not the toughest, of all the Open Championship venues. Many of the world's top players found the length of the course, the narrow fairways and the severity of the rough presented a daunting examination, which most of them failed to pass. With a superb new hotel now located directly behind the 18th green and 1st tee, and the course fully restored to first-class condition, Carnoustie now looks well and truly established once again on the list of Open Championship courses.

Visually it could not be more intimidating. The land is very cheerless, furnished with scrubs, scrapes and ditches. There are none of the moonscape dunes that you associate with the great Open courses; neither is it a traditional out-and-back links. Instead, the severity of the course is entirely governed by the strength of the wind and the height of the rough. Players have to hit the ground running at Carnoustie, requiring a long iron to a hidden green at the 1st, and then having to avoid a bunker in the middle of the fairway at the long par-4 2nd. There is a brief respite until the 6th, a par-5 with out-of-bounds all the way up the left and, once again, strategic bunkers placed in the middle of the fairway. From there, you need to thread a line through the out-of-bounds and a burn to set up a pitch to the green.

But it's the closing holes for which Carnoustie is famed, starting with the 15th, a 460-yard par-4 swinging spectacularly around a rolling ridge. The 16th is, wait for it, a 248-yard par-3, followed by the 17th, where you face a drive to a fairway that is almost completely surrounded by a stream. Both the 17th and the 18th, which cross the stream twice, provide a very un-links-style finish but are excellent for matchplay, producing exciting finishes, as the world witnessed during the thrilling play-off for the 1999 Open Championship. Carnoustie's regeneration gives the links a very fresh feel. Play it before it's too late.

Secretary: Mr E. J. C. Smith   Tel: 01241 853789
                                          Fax: 01241 852720
Professional: Mr L. Vannet   Tel: 01241 853789

Playing: Midweek: round £52.00; day n/a. Weekend: round
                   £52.00; day n/a. Handicap certificate required.

Facilities: Bar: None. Food: Full facilities from April 1999.

Comments: Best in the country ... Ultimate test of golf overrides lack
                   of facilities ... Course only lacks playability ... Need to
                   cut back rough for amateurs ... Don't play this beast in
                   any more than a breeze ... What a course, a must ... A
                   real education although expensive ... The No. 1 in
                   Scotland ... New hotel will improve the facilities no end
                   ... Most difficult I've played ... Great test – in the
                   Portmarnock class ... No dunes, no long rough – it's the
                   design that is so punishing ... Greens are the killer ...
                   Finish is the toughest anywhere.

The Gleneagles Hotel (King's)   ★★★★★

Auchterarder, PH3 1NF
Nearest main town: Perth

If you think of Scottish golf courses as wild and unkempt, then think
again. Gleneagles will blow away any preconceptions you might have.
There are four courses at this exclusive golf and hotel bolt-hole, all
beautifully manicured with a very modern feel. The King's Course is the
best of them all and few come away without falling in love with this very
sensuous and natural course.

The King's lays claim to be the best inland course in Scotland, and
the claim is founded on very solid arguments. It is kept in consistently
superb condition, but not even the heather-clad Grampian Mountains
which form the backdrop to the course, or the silver birch and rowan,
can persuade you that this is a victory of style over content. There are
eighteen very individual holes here, providing a varied technical test.
There are drives from elevated tees to camber fairways, approach shots
to elevated greens, sweeping plateau doglegs, angled greens, downhill
approaches and more.

Many of the best holes come towards the end of the round. There's
the driveable short par-4 14th, where you can gamble on setting up an
eagle or birdie, the plunge approach to the par-4 15th and the par-3
16th played to an angled green protected by an enormous hill covered

in wild grasses. The 17th swings around the side of a hill to a sloping, elevated green and, finally, the par-5 18th, the first half of which is a very natural roller-coaster fairway.

What will strike you about the King's Course is the shaping and artistry of the holes. The fairways and greens have very curvy lines, and even the bunkers seem to draw your vision. With the bushes and grassy hills teeming with wildlife, it's a riveting experience. And if you're staying at the Gleneagles Hotel, a standard bearer for service and welcome in Scotland, you will truly be the envy of your golfing compatriots.

Secretary:	Miss H. Edment	Tel: 01764 663543
		Fax: 01764 694383
Professional:	Mr G. Schofield	Tel: 01764 663543

Playing: Midweek: round £85.00; day £100.00. Weekend: round n/a; day n/a. Handicap certificate required.

Facilities: Bar: 11am–11pm. Food: Breakfast, lunch and dinner from 7am–10pm. Bar snacks.

Comments: Famed Gleneagles quality … Palatial course … A haven for wildlife … Sculpted masterpiece with elements of all the classics … Can get windy … A right royal experience … On a fine spring morning, it is paradise … Fantastic … Nothing better, but at a price … Outstanding in every way, only the cost is off-putting … Beautiful, natural layout with fabulous practice facilities … Perfect in every way…Played like a rabbit, would like to go back and play well … Heaven in the Glens … Everything is excellent … Layout and course condition second to none.

Alyth Golf Club ★★★

Pitcrocknie, Alyth, PH11 8HF
Nearest main town: Dundee

Secretary:	Mr J. Docherty	Tel: 01828 632268
		Fax: 01828 633491
Professional:	Mr T. Melville	Tel: 01828 632411
		Fax 01828 632411

Playing: Midweek: round £20.00; day £30.00. Weekend: round £25.00; day £40.00. Handicap certificate required.

Facilities: Bar: 11am–11pm. Food: Bar snacks. Dinner by arrangement.

Comments: Beautifully looked after, hard-to-master course ... Well-protected greens ... Does not get recognition it deserves ... Variety in abundance ... Far from straightforward parkland course ... In the shadow of a nearby classic links.

Arbroath Golf Course ★★

Elliott, Arbroath, PD11 2PE
Nearest main town: Arbroath

Secretary: Mr Scott. Milne   Tel: 01241 875837
                                       Fax: 01241 875837
Professional: Mr J. Lindsay Stewart PGA   Tel: 01241 875837
                                       Fax 01241 875837

Playing: Midweek: round £16.00; day £20.00. Weekend: round £20.00; day £30.00. Handicap certificate required.

Facilities: Bar: 11am–11pm. Food: 9am–8pm

Comments: Short but testing, especially when the wind blows in from the North Sea ... Perfect introduction to Scottish links courses before you decide to take on some of the real monsters! ... Course really gets going from the 7th, Practice your bunker shots before you play here ... Clubhouse facilities could be improved.

Auchterarder Golf Club

Ochil Road, Auchterarder, PH3 1LS
Nearest main town: Auchterarder

Secretary: Mr W. M. Campbell   Tel: 01764 662804
                                    Fax: 01764 662804
Professional: Mr G. Baxter   Tel: 01764 663711
                                    Fax 01764 663711

Playing: Midweek: round £18.00; day £26.00. Weekend: round £24.00; day £36.00. Handicap certificate required.

Facilities: Bar: 11am–11pm. Food: Lunch and dinner from 11am–9pm. Bar snacks.

Comments: Great holiday golf ... Not too long or demanding ... Made to feel very welcome ... A mini Gleneagles ... No par-5s but still very enjoyable ... Good bar.

Blairgowrie Golf Club (Rosemount)   ★★★★

Rosemount, Blairgowie, PH10 6LG
Nearest main town: Perth

Secretary:	Mr J. N. Simpson	Tel: 01250 872622
		Fax: 01250 875451
Professional:	Mr C. Dernie	Tel: 01250 873116
		Fax 01250 873116

Playing: Midweek: round £50.00; day £60.00. Weekend: round £55.00; day £75.00. Handicap certificate required.

Facilities: Bar: 11am–11pm. Food: Lunch and dinner from 10am–9pm. Bar snacks.

Comments: Setting and presentation could not be bettered ... Greatly overrated ... Unique in Scotland but not a patch on Sunningdale, Liphook, Swinley Forest, West Sussex ... Expensive with poor facilities for visitors ... If I lived in Scotland this is the club I would join ... Visitors are not made to feel welcome ... Unique in Scotland ... Each hole separated from the others ... Great flora and fauna.

Blairgowrie Golf Club (Lansdowne)   ★★

Rosemount, Blairgowrie, PH10 6LG
Nearest main town: Perth

Secretary:	Mr J. N. Simpson	Tel: 01250 872622
		Fax: 01250 875451
Professional:	Mr C. Dernie	Tel: 01250 873116
		Fax 01250 873116

Playing: Midweek: round £40.00; day £60.00. Weekend: round £45.00; day £75.00. Handicap certificate required.

Facilities: Bar: 11am–11pm. Food: Lunch and dinner from 10am–9pm. Bar snacks.

Comments: Like Rosemount, greatly overrated but even less fun to play ... Trademark Alliss/Thomas design ... Very narrow driving areas ... Couldn't pick which course I preferred ... Somewhat monotonous layout ... Great clubhouse.

Braehead Golf Club ★★

Cambus, Alloa, FK10 2NT
Nearest main town: Alloa

Secretary:	Mr P. MacMichael	Tel: 01259 725766
		Fax: 01259 725766
Professional:	Mr P. Brookes	Tel: 01259 722078
		Fax 01259 720731

Playing: Midweek: round £18.50; day £24.50. Weekend: round £24.50; day £32.50. Handicap certificate required.

Facilities: Bar: 11am–11pm. Food: Lunch and dinner from 10am–9pm. Bar snacks.

Comments: Some testing par-3s, particularly the 14th ... Not much to look at ... Nice design, fair to all standards.

Brechin Golf & Squash Club ★★

Trinity, by Brechin, Brechin, DD9 7PD
Nearest main town: Brechin

Secretary:	Mr Ian A. Jardine	Tel: 01356 622383
		Fax: 01356 626925
Professional:	Mr Stephen Rennie	Tel: 01356 625270

Playing: Midweek: round £17.00; day £25.00. Weekend: round £22.00; day £30.00. Handicap certificate required.

Facilities: Bar: 11am–11pm. Food: 11am–9pm.

Comments: Greens are among the best I've played on ... Some of the holes have been there for over a hundred years ... My pick of the bunch are the 10th and 17th ... Putting surfaces very quick and true, but difficult to read. Midweek package – £28.00 for two rounds and full catering (groups of eight or more, Monday to Friday).

Buchanan Castle Golf Club ★★★

Drymen, G63 0HY
Nearest main town: Glasgow

Secretary:	Mr R. Kinsella	Tel: 01360 660307
Professional:	Mr K. Baxter	Tel: 01360 660330
		Fax 01360 660330

Playing: Midweek: round £30.00; day £40.00. Weekend: round £30.00; day £40.00. Handicap certificate required.

Facilities: Bar: 11am–11pm. Food: Lunch and dinner from 10am–9pm. Bar snacks.

Comments: Very welcoming ... Loch Lomond is nearby ... Plenty of water in play ... Nice mix of natural hazards ... Conditioning out of the top drawer ... Shamefully under-rated.

Callander Golf Club   ★★★

Aveland Road, Callander, FK17 8EN
Nearest main town: Callander

Secretary: Mr D. Allan   Tel: 01877 330090
(Manager)   Fax: 01877 330062
Professional: To be appointed.

Playing: Midweek: round £18.00; day £26.00. Weekend: round £31.00; day £36.00. Handicap certificate required.

Facilities: Bar: 11am–11pm. Food: Lunch and dinner from 10am–9pm. Bar snacks.

Comments: Good course from back tees but visitors only play about 4,000 yards from front tees or bits of fairway ... Nice test in the Trossachs ... Design by Tom Morris Snr ... Members too protective of course ... Very poor value for visitors.

Camperdown Golf Course   ★★

Camperdown Park, Dundee, DD4 9BX
Nearest main town: Dundee

Secretary: Mr R. Gordon   Tel: 01382 814445 –
Bookings 01382 623398
Professional: Mr R. Brown

Playing: Midweek: round £15.00; day n/a. Weekend: round n/a; day n/a. Handicap certificate required.

Facilities: Bar: None. Food: None.

Comments: Excellent parkland style layout with fairways running through avenues of tall mature pine trees ... Grass on the greens was a little long but really enjoyed the variety of holes ... Must be one of Scotland's best value pay-and-play courses ... Superb setting in the Camperdown Estate ... Clubhouse facilities could be improved ... Must be the smallest pro shop in the country ... Cracking short holes, especially enjoyed the 4th and the 17th which is around 160 yards and played uphill ... Tee shot on the par-5 10th, is the scariest on the course ... Fairly hilly but not overly tiring to walk.

Carnoustie Burnside   ★★★

Links Parade, Carnoustie, St Andrews, DD7 7JE
Nearest main town: Dundee

Secretary: Mr E. J. C. Smith   Tel: 01241 855344 (Starters)
                                            Tel: 01241 853789 (Bookings)
                                            Fax: 01241 852720

Professional: None.

Playing: Midweek: round £20.00; day £20.00. Weekend: round £20.00; day £20.00. Sat after 2.00pm, Sun after 11.30am. Handicap certificate required.

Facilities: Bar: n/a. Food: n/a.

Comments: Always in the shadow of the Championship course but a really good test of golf in its own right ... Every bit as good as the Open venue it runs alongside, only shorter ... Short 5th is a really testing hole which is almost completely surrounded by the famous Barry Burn ... Great finishing stretch with the Barry Burn a major threat in the final two holes ... General condition of the course was excellent ... Much cheaper to play than the big course and much more fun for the average player ... Outstanding par-3 holes.

Crieff Golf Club   ★★★★★

Perth Road, Crieff, PH7 3LR
Nearest main town: Perth

Secretary: Mr J. S. Miller   Tel: 01764 652397
                                            Fax: 01764 655093
Professional: Mr D. J. W. Murchie   Tel: 01764 652909

Playing: Midweek: round £20.00; day £34.00. Weekend: round £28.00; day n/a. Handicap certificate required.

Facilities: Bar: 11am–10pm. Food: Lunch and dinner from 10am–9pm.

Comments: Parkland course where every shot needs careful thought ... Built on the side of a hill ... People are what make the club ... Sloping lies *ad nauseam* ... Only one blind hole and long par-4s ... Best golf experience in Scotland ... Nine in the morning, 18 in the afternoon – perfect.

Downfield Golf Club   ★★★★

Turnberry Avenue, Dundee, DD2 3QP
Nearest main town: Dundee

Secretary: Mr B. D. Liddle   Tel: 01382 825595
                                          Fax: 01382 813111
Professional: Mr K. S. Hutton   Tel: 01382 889246

Playing: Midweek: round £26.00; day £36.00. Weekend: round £31.00; day n/a. Handicap certificate required.

Facilities: Bar: 11am–11pm. Food: Lunch and dinner from 10am–9pm. Bar snacks.

Comments: Slightly disappointed at condition on last visit as it is normally top class ... Best inland course I have played ... A bit of everything here ... Bit pricey ... Good practice and pro facilities ... Not well known outside Scotland ... Heavily wooded inland course ... Not what you expect in Scotland ... Don't miss it.

Edzell Golf Club   ★★★★

High Street, Edzell, DD9 7TF
Nearest main town: Brechin

Secretary: Mr I. G. Farquhar   Tel: 01356 647283
                                          Fax: 01356 648094
Professional: Mr A. J. Webster   Tel: 01356 648462
                                          Fax 01356 648884

Playing: Midweek: round £21.00; day £31.00. Weekend: round £27.00; day £41.00. Handicap certificate required.

Facilities: Bar: 11am–11pm. Food: Lunch and dinner from 10am–9pm. Bar snacks.

Comments: Highly regarded but not all it's made out to be ... Would not rush back ... A course that combines challenge and chasm ... Friendliest club in Scotland ... One of Scotland's best kept secrets ... Gets wet in winter ... Outstanding finishing hole and great greens ... Picturesque, interesting and friendly ... Small, compact course with tiny greens and quaint holes ... A treat ... Hospitality first class.

Forfar Golf Club   ★★★

Cunninghill, Arbroath Road, Forfar, DD8 2RL
Nearest main town: Forfar

Secretary: Mr W. Baird   Tel: 01307 463773
                                         Fax: 01307 468495
Professional: Mr P. McNiven   Tel: 01307 465683
                                         Fax 01307 465683

Playing: Midweek: round £17.00; day £17.00. Weekend: round £25.00; day £30.00. Handicap certificate required.

Facilities: Bar: 11am–11pm. Food: Lunch and dinner from noon–8pm. Bar snacks.

Comments: Tree-lined course always in immaculate condition ... A joy to play ... First-class condition ... Layout suspect but condition superb ... A little short, but undeniably sweet.

Green Hotel Golf Course   ★★★

The Muirs, Kinross, KY13 8AS
Nearest main town: Perth

Secretary: Mr C. Browne   Tel: 01577 863407
                                         Fax: 01577 863180
Professional: Mr S. Geraghty   Tel: 01577 865125
                                         Fax 01577 864296

Playing: Midweek: round £17.00; day £27.00. Weekend: round £27.00; day £37.00. Handicap certificate required.

Facilities: Bar: 11am–11pm. Food: All day – coffee and bacon rolls for early tee-off, soup and filled rolls and high tea.

Comments: Wonderful secluded setting. It's hard to believe you are only a few minutes' drive from the busy Perth to Edinburgh motorway ... Two excellent courses to choose from ... Generously wide fairways flanked by wonderful variety of mature trees ... Loved the par-3s ... Big greens in excellent condition.

King James VI Golf Club   ★★★

Moncreiffe Island, Perth, PH2 8NR
Nearest main town: Perth

Secretary: Mrs Helen Blair   Tel: 01738 445132
Professional: Mr Andrew Crerar   Tel: 01738 632460

Playing: Midweek: round £17.00; day n/a. Weekend: round £20.00 – Sundays only; day n/a. Handicap certificate required.

Facilities: Bar: 11am–11pm. Food: All day.

Comments: Unique and attractive setting on what is virtually an island in the middle of the River Tay. Very flat but still interesting ... A little daunting at first with all that water surrounding the course ... Fairways and tees in excellent condition.

Kirriemuir Golf Club   ★★

Northmuir, Kirriemuir, DD8 4PN
Nearest main town: Dundee

Secretary: Mr C. Garry   Tel: 01575 573317
                                            Fax: 01575 574608
Professional: Mrs K. Ellis   Tel: 01575 573317

Playing: Midweek: round £18.00; day £24.00. Weekend: round n/a; day n/a. Handicap certificate required.

Facilities: Bar: 11am–11pm. Food: Bar snacks.

Comments: Interesting and enjoyable but not that difficult ... Views of the Angus glens ... Short but not that sweet ... Better to be found in the area.

Letham Grange Golf Club   ★★★

Letham Grange, Colliston, DD11 4RL
Nearest main town: Arbroath

Secretary:	Miss C. Grainger	Tel: 01241 890377
		Fax: 01241 890414
Professional:	Mr S. Moir	Tel: 01241 890377

Playing: Midweek: round £27.50; day £40.00. Weekend: round £35.00; day £55.00. Handicap certificate required.

Facilities: Bar: 11am–11pm. Food: Breakfast, lunch and dinner from 9am–11pm. Bar snacks.

Comments: Meant to be a Scottish Augusta but far from it ... Very un-Scottish course but good fun ... Target golf with a few blind shots thrown in ... New course complements the superior Old well ... Nice change from links golf ... Tranquil setting for this US-style course ... Excellent facilities and a course to match ... Felt very peaceful and golf was fun ... Had a great laugh ... One of Donald Steel's best courses ... Water hazards a constant peril ... Prefer it to all those links.

Monifieth Golf Links (Medal)   ★★★★

Medal Starter's Box, Princes Street, Monifieth, DD5 4AW
Nearest main town: Dundee

Secretary:	Mr H. R. Nicoll	Tel: 01382 532767
		Fax: 01382 535553
Professional:	Mr I. McLeod	Tel: 01382 532945

Playing: Midweek: round £26.00; day £36.00. Weekend: round £30.00; day n/a. Handicap certificate required.

Facilities: Bar: 11am–11pm. Food: Breakfast, lunch and dinner from 7am–10pm. Bar snacks.

Comments: A links with a friendly membership, unfriendly wind and lovely well-tended greens and fairways ... Straightforward links ... Near Carnoustie ... Very exposed.

Monifieth Golf Links (Ashludie)   ★★★

Medal Starter's Box, Princes Street, Monifieth, DD5 4AW
Nearest main town: Dundee

Secretary:	Mr H. R. Nicoll	Tel: 01382 532767
		Fax: 01382 535553
Professional:	Mr I. McLeod	Tel: 01382 532945

Playing: Midweek: round £15.00; day £21.00. Weekend: round £16.00; day £24.00. Handicap certificate required.

Facilities: Bar: 11am–11pm. Food: Breakfast, lunch and dinner from 7am–10pm. Bar snacks.

Comments: Don't come to Monifieth for this one ... Short links of some character ... Ticket to play both is good value.

Montrose Links Trust   ★★★★★

Traill Drive, Montrose, DD10 8SW
Nearest main town: Montrose

Secretary:	Mrs M. Stewart	Tel: 01674 672932
		Fax: 01674 671800
Professional:	Mr K. Stables	Tel: 01674 672634

Playing: Midweek: round £22.00; day £33.00. Weekend: round £30.00; day £45.00. Handicap certificate required.

Facilities: Bar: 11am–11pm. Food: Lunch from noon–8pm.

Comments: Forgotten stern links that is part of the life of the town ... Superb course ... Tricky – just what you would expect from a links ... Good value and a joy to play ... Golf played here since the 16th century ... Historic master-piece ... A links legend ... Deep bunkers, springy turf, towering sand dunes.

Murrayshall Hotel Golf Club   ★★★

Murrayshall, New Scone, Perth, PH2 7PH
Nearest main town: Perth

Secretary:	Mr A. Bryan	Tel: 01738 551171
	(Manager)	Fax: 01738 552595
Professional:	Mr A. T. Reid	Tel: 01738 552784

Playing: Midweek: round £22.00; day £32.00. Weekend: round £27.00; day £40.00. Handicap certificate required.

Facilities: Bar: 11am–11pm. Food: Breakfast, lunch and dinner from 7am–10pm.

Comments: Some uninteresting holes on a course in average condition ... Take three trees out of the middle of the fairways
and this would be a great course ... Difficult to find any
faults ... Greens well protected and pins difficult to attack.

Panmure Golf Club   ★★★

Barry, Carnoustie, DD7 7RT
Nearest main town: Carnoustie

Secretary: Maj. G. W. Paton   Tel: 01241 855120
                                         Fax: 01241 859737
Professional: Mr N. Mackintosh   Tel: 01241 852460

Playing: Midweek: round £30.00; day £45.00. Weekend: round
                   £30.00; day £45.00. Handicap certificate required.

Facilities: Bar: 11am–11pm. Food: Lunch from 10am–9pm. Bar
                   snacks.

Comments: Weekend play on Sundays only ... Members not keen on
                   visitors playing their course or using their clubhouse –
                   just like Elie ... Complements nearby Carnoustie and
                   Monifieth ... Bump-and-run golf ... Awkward bounces,
                   narrow fairways, rough devastating ... Short but feels
                   like 7,000 yards in the wind.

Pitlochry Golf Club   ★★★

Golf Course Road, Pitlochry, PH16 5QY
Nearest main town: Perth

Secretary: Mr D. C. M. McKenzie Tel: 01796 472114
                                         Fax: 01796 473599
Professional: Mr G. Hampton   Tel: 01796 472792

Playing: Midweek: round £14.00; day £21.00. Weekend: round
                   £18.00; day £27.00. Handicap certificate required.

Facilities: Bar: 11am–11pm. Food: Lunch and dinner from
                   10am–9pm. Bar snacks.

Comments: Stunning setting and top value for money ... A delight to
                   play ... First four holes go straight uphill and are
                   exhausting ... Meanders back down and is worth a visit
                   ... Hard opener and gets easier ... Up hill and down
                   dale at this course on the side of a mountain ... Second
                   shot to the 4th is a thriller ... Plunging approach shots
                   and driveable par-4s, great fun.

Stirling Golf Club   ★★

Queen's Road, Stirling, FK8 3AA
Nearest main town: Stirling

Secretary: Mr W. C. McArthur   Tel: 01786 464098
                                         Fax: 01786 450748
Professional: Mr I. Collins   Tel: 01786 471490

Playing: Midweek: round £20.00; day £30.00. Weekend: round
                  n/a; day n/a. Handicap certificate required.

Facilities: Bar: 11am–11pm. Food: Breakfast, lunch and dinner
                  from 10am–9pm. Bar snacks.

Comments: Non-descript rolling parkland course ... Usually in good
                  condition ... Stirling Castle broods over the course ...
                  Surprisingly difficult.

Taymouth Castle Golf Course   ★★★

Taymouth Castle Estate, Kenmore, PH15 2NT
Nearest main town: Aberfeldy 5 miles

Secretary: Mr Robert Smith   Tel: 01887 829771
Professional: Mr Alex Marshall   Tel: 01887 820910

Playing: Midweek: round £20.00; day £30.00. Weekend: round
                  £24.00; day £38.00. Handicap certificate required.

Facilities: Bar: 11am – late; 12.30pm – late Sundays. Food: All
                  day.

Comments: Delight to play ... Loved the big wide fairways and flat
                  greens ... Wonderful setting in great condition ... Hard
                  to beat for a relaxed round of golf. Some fine holes,
                  especially on the homeward run ... Scottish golf at its
                  very best ... Very friendly staff in the clubhouse ...
                  Clubhouse available from 8am until late.

The Gleneagles Hotel (Monarch)   ★★★★

Auchterarder, PH3 1NF
Nearest main town: Perth

Secretary: Miss H. Edment   Tel: 01764 663543
                                        Fax: 01764 694383
Professional: Mr G. Schofield   Tel: 01764 6635543

Playing: Midweek: round £85.00; day £100.00. Weekend: round n/a; day n/a. Handicap certificate required.

Facilities: Bar: 11am–11pm. Food: Breakfast, lunch and dinner from 7am–10pm. Bar snacks.

Comments: A fantastic set-up with course presentation out of this world ... Only snag way too pricey ... Some good holes but overall a bit of a let-down ... Poor ground in places and rather ordinary greens ... Stunning US-style course not normally associated with Scotland ... Excellent presentation and condition.

The Gleneagles Hotel (Queens)   ★★★★

Auchterarder, PH3 1NF
Nearest main town: Perth

Secretary: Miss H. Edment   Tel: 01764 663543
                                      Fax: 01764 694383
Professional: Mr G. Schofield   Tel: 01764 663543

Playing: Midweek: round £85.00; day £100.00. Weekend: round n/a; day n/a. Handicap certificate required.

Facilities: Bar: 11am–11pm. Food: Breakfast, lunch and dinner from 7am–10pm. Bar snacks.

Comments: A good course in its own right ... Inevitably overshadowed by neighbours ... Condition a match for anything around ... Easiest course here ... Facilities just out of this world ... Surprisingly good ... Enjoyed it immensely ... Not far behind the other two.

Aberdeen & Grampian

Cruden Bay Golf Club

Cruden Bay, Peterhead, AB42 0NN
Nearest main town: Peterhead

It's often said of Cruden Bay that no present-day designer in the world would have the cheek to design such a quirky, eccentric course as this. For instance, the 14th has no view of the fairway from the tee, or the green from the fairway; the 15th is a blind par-3; and the 3rd and the 8th were seemingly thrown in without much thought, as par-4s well short of 300 yards.

Whether you view Cruden Bay as a hoot, or the epitome of links golf, you can't fail to be impressed by the location. Such was its desirability, a luxurious hotel occupied the site from the turn of the century to 1947, to which the rich and famous came to be spoilt – or more likely to play Cruden Bay. The 'Palace in the Sandhills', as it was tagged, was knocked down, and so, having had its turn in the limelight, Cruden Bay was shuffled off stage.

At least this saved Cruden Bay from being lumbered with the cachet of, say, Ballybunion. It is not overcrowded with visitors and its condition is normally good. Indeed, it seems to get better with age, the sandhills standing prouder, the fairways gnarled and more resistant to the footprints of holiday golfers. Even Cruden Bay beach, where the sands are 'as smooth and firm as the floor of a cathedral' seem to act as a stronger barrier between the North Sea and the course itself.

You can see it all from the clubhouse, laid out below you. This view, where you can see the holes threading their way through the dunes, really sets the adrenalin flowing, and you can only excitedly rush to the 1st tee from there. You'll be terrified, amused, humbled and downright knackered when you finish, but, most importantly of all, you'll remember Cruden Bay fondly.

Secretary: Mrs R. Pittendrigh   Tel: 01779 812285
                                      Fax: 01779 812945
Professional: Mr R. G. Stewart   Tel: 01779 812414
                                      Fax 01779 812414

Playing: Midweek: round £35.00; day £50.00. Weekend: round £45.00; day n/a. Handicap certificate required.

Facilities: Bar: 11am–11pm. Food: Breakfast, lunch and dinner from 9am–10pm. Bar snacks.

Comments: Tough links between high sand dunes ... Lovely views over the bay ... Experience not to be forgotten ... Wonderful location ... A true rival to courses across the UK ... Full of surprises, every hole is memorable ... Wonderfully peaceful and natural place to play ... Any number of exciting and unusual shots ... Holes 4–8 are great ... A real links course apart from one silly hole – magnificent ... View from 10th tee is the best in golf ... The best ... Who needs Pebble Beach? ... Outstanding scenery ... It's got the lot ... The most difficult links course around ... Everything you would want from a golf course ... A tactician's course ... Gobsmacked ... Unbelievable.

Aboyne Golf Club   ★★

Formaston Park, Aboyne, AB34 5HP
Nearest main town: Aberdeen

Secretary: Mrs M. MacLean   Tel: 013398 87078
                                        Fax: 013398 87078
Professional: Mr I. Wright   Tel: 013398 86328

Playing: Midweek: round £18.00; day £24.00. Weekend: round £22.00; day £28.00. Handicap certificate required.

Facilities: Bar: 11am–11pm. Food: Lunch from 10am–3pm.

Comments: Good pro shop ... Was impressed with condition ... Very flat and little definition ... Not bad value for fair quality golf ... Shoot the lights out ... Accesible first-time course ... Very straightforward.

Ballater Golf Club   ★★★

Victoria Road, Ballater, AB35 5QX
Nearest main town: Aberdeen (40 miles)

Secretary: Mr A. E. (Sandy)   Tel: 01339 755567
                    Barclay   Fax: 01339 755057
Professional: Mr Bill Yule   Tel: 01339 755658
                                          Fax 01339 755057

Playing: Midweek: round £18.00; day £27.00. Weekend: round £21.00; day £31.00. Handicap certificate required.

Facilities: Bar: 11am – midnight. Food: 10.00am – 8.00pm (unless prior arrangements are made).

Comments: Super setting that must be among the most scenic in this part of the country ... Short 3rd takes some beating. It plays uphill to a well-bunkered green that falls away steeply on the left. I couldn't wait to play the course again in the afternoon ... Greens in good condition but not what you would call lightening fast ... Not too long and really enjoyable for the less talented golfer ... When the sun shines there is no finer or more tranquil spot to play golf ... Everyone was so friendly and helpful.

Braemar Golf Club   ★★★

Cluniebank Road, Braemar, AB35 5XX
Nearest main town: Ballater

Secretary: Mr J. Pennet   Tel: 013397 41618
Professional: None.

Playing: Midweek: round £13.00; day £18.00. Weekend: round £16.00; day £21.00. Handicap certificate required.

Facilities: Bar: 11am–11pm. Food: Bar snacks.

Comments: Enchanting for many reasons ... Must have some of the most difficult par-3s and easiest par-4s anywhere ... Wonderful setting for great golf ... Beautiful scenery ... Short course with good par-3s.

Cullen Golf Club

The Links, Cullen, AB56 2UU
Nearest main town: Buckie

Secretary: Mr L. I. G. Findlay   Tel: 01542 840685
Professional: None.

Playing: Midweek: round £10.00; day £15.00. Weekend: round £13.00; day £18.00. Handicap certificate required.

Facilities: Bar: 11am–11pm. Food: Bar snacks.

Comments: Eccentric little links ... So natural, pity the course can't be extended ... Balls can bounce off the rocks ... Beach can come into play for wayward shots ... An unusual golfing day out.

Deeside Golf Club   ★★★

Bieldside, Aberdeen, AB15 9DL
Nearest main town: Aberdeen

Secretary:	Mr A. G. Macdonald	Tel: 01224 869457
		Fax: 01224 869457
Professional:	Mr F. J. Courts	Tel: 01224 861041
		Fax 01224 861041

Playing: Midweek: round £25.00; day n/a. Weekend: round £30.00; day n/a. Handicap certificate required.

Facilities: Bar: 11am–11pm. Food: Lunch and dinner from 10am–9pm. Bar snacks.

Comments: Quality club ... Riverside course with brooks and streams ... All sorts of dangers lurking here ... Not long but not short on interest.

Duff House Royal Golf Club   ★★★★

The Barnyards, Banff, AB45 3SX
Nearest main town: Buckie

Secretary:	Mrs J. Maison	Tel: 01261 812062
		Fax: 01261 812224
Professional:	Mr R. S. Strachan	Tel: 01261 812075
		Fax 01261 812075

Playing: Midweek: round £18.00; day £24.00. Weekend: round £25.00; day £30.00. Handicap certificate required.

Facilities: Bar: 11am–11pm. Food: Lunch and dinner from 10am–9pm. Bar snacks.

Comments: Cracking value for an interesting, challenging and subtle course of substance ... Could not fault the course ... Greens like silk and food that says 'More please' and it's in Scotland! ... Never too busy ... Great condition ... Course protected by tricky greens ... Exceptional greens.

Fraserburgh Golf Club   ★★

Philorth, Fraserburgh, AB4 8TL
Nearest main town: Peterhead

Secretary:	Mr D. J. Bond	Tel: 01346 516616
Professional:	None.	

Playing: Midweek: round £15.00; day £20.00. Weekend: round £20.00; day £25.00. Handicap certificate required.

Facilities: Bar: 11am–11pm – seven days. Food: Full catering facilities.

Comments: A different challenge on almost every hole ... Really testing even when the wind is not blowing ... Hit it on the fairways, or be sure you bring plenty of golf balls ... Golf at its most natural, with fairways running between huge sandhills ... Excellent greens.

Hazelhead Golf Course   ★★

Hazelhead Park, Aberdeen, AB15 8BD
Nearest main town: Aberdeen

Secretary: Mr William MacKay   Tel: 01224 315747
Professional: Mr Alastair Smith   Tel: 01224 321830

Playing: Midweek: round £9.00 – winter rates are lower; day n/a. Weekend: round £11.25 – winter rates are lower; day n/a. Handicap certificate required.

Facilities: Bar: 11am–2.30pm and 5pm–11pm. Food: Bar snacks and meals available during opening time.

Comments: There are three public golf courses at Hazelhead with No. 1 being the best of the bunch ... An interesting parkland layout running through a tree-lined estate ... Not too tight and can flatter your game if you are playing well ... Originally designed by the famous golf course architect, Alistair MacKenzie, who also created Augusta National ... Good value for money ... Toughest hole on the course is the 435-yard 14th with out of bounds on the right and trees on the left ... Best of the four short holes is the 177-yard 5th, where the tee shot has to carry a deep valley directly in front of the green ... Greens suffered last year from very wet winter and spring.

Huntly Golf Club   ★★

Cooper Park, Huntly, AB54 4SH
Nearest main town: Huntly

Secretary: Mr E. A. Stott   Tel: 01466 792360
                                          (Bookings 01466 792643)

Professional: Mr Sandy Aird   Tel: 01466 794181
                                          (Lessons by arrangement)

Playing: Midweek: round £12.00; day £18.00. Weekend: round
                 £18.00 (weekly ticket available at £65.00); day £24.00.
                 Handicap certificate required.

Facilities: Bar: 10am–11pm summer; closed from 2pm–
                 6pm Mon to Fri; winter open all day Saturday and Sunday.
                 Food: Bar snacks and meals available – seasonal timing.

Comments: Great combination of rolling fairways running through
                 wonderful stands of mature trees ... Look out for that
                 troublesome little burn that features on at least four
                 holes ... A slicer's delight because most of the trouble is
                 on the left side ... Glimpses of Huntly Castle through the
                 trees as the second hole provides a memorable start to
                 the round ... Clubhouse newly refurbished and facilities
                 are excellent, they claim to offer the cheapest "dram" in
                 Scotland at 75p a shot!

Kemnay Golf Club   ★★

Monymusk Road, Kemnay, AB51 5RA
Nearest main town: Aberdeen

Secretary: Mr B. Robertson   Tel: 01467 643746
                                          Fax: 01467 643746
Professional: Mr R. MacDonald   Tel: 01467 642225

Playing: Midweek: round £16.00; day £20.00. Weekend: round
                  £18.00; day £22.00. Handicap certificate required.

Facilities: Bar: 11am–11pm. Food: Bar snacks. Dinner by
                  arrangement.

Comments: Undulating and exciting ... Always easy to get a round
                  ... Excellent views ... Fairly ordinary parkland.

King's Links Golf Course

Golf Road, King's Links, Aberdeen, AB24 5QB
Nearest main town: Aberdeen

Secretary: Mr B. Davidson   Tel: 01224 632269
Professional: None.

Playing: Midweek: round £9.00; day £11.25. Weekend: round n/a; day n/a. Handicap certificate required.

Facilities: Bar: n/a. Food: n/a.

Comments: Golf has been played on the ground where the course stands today from around the 16th century ... Good value for money ... Public course but in good condition with some really excellent holes ... Good opportunity to sort out your swing faults and pick up a few tips at the nearby King's Links Golf Centre, which is one of the best practice and teaching facilities in Scotland.

Kintore Golf Club ★★

Kintore, AB51 0UR
Nearest main town: Aberdeen

Secretary: Mrs V. Graham   Tel: 01467 632631
Professional: None.

Playing: Midweek: round £11; day £15.00. Weekend: round £16.00; day £20.00. Handicap certificate required.

Facilities: Bar: 11am–11pm. Food: Lunch from noon–2pm. Dinner from 6pm–9pm.

Comments: Moorland/woodland course of character ... Excellent round rate for this charming club ... Nothing special ... Made welcome.

Murcar Golf Club ★★★

Bridge of Don, Aberdeen, AB23 8BD
Nearest main town: Aberdeen

Secretary: Mr D. Corstorphine   Tel: 01224 704354
                                      Fax: 01224 704354
Professional: Mr G. Forbes   Tel: 01224 704370

Playing: Midweek: round £30.00; day £40.00. Weekend: round £35.00; day £45.00. Handicap certificate required.

Facilities: Bar: 11am–11pm. Food: Lunch and dinner from 10am–10pm. Bar snacks.

Comments: The total package ... Fantastic setting ... Great fun (avoid a windy day, though) ... .Great short par-4s ... Improved condition.

Newburgh-on-Ythan   ★★★

Beach Road, Newburgh, Ellon, AB41 6BE
Nearest main town: Aberdeen

Secretary: Mrs Vivien Geoghegan   Tel: 01358 789058
                                            Fax: 01358 789956
Professional: None.

Playing: Midweek: round £16.00; day £21.00. Weekend: round
                    £21.00; day £26.00. Handicap certificate required.

Facilities: Bar: Seasonal. Food: New clubhouse opens July 2000
                    or by request in advance.

Comments: Played every hole a hundred times but still look forward
                    to seeing them ... Founded in the 19th century and
                    reeks of history ... Forgotten course ... Lovely club with
                    course to be proud of ... First impressions are not all
                    that impressive, but persevere. The further you play the
                    better the course gets ... Unusual but enjoyable combi-
                    nation of links and pasture land ... Layout starts on
                    higher ground then sweeps down to run alongside the
                    River Ythan (pronounced 'eye thin') ... Good test, espe-
                    cially over the back nine.

Newmacher Golf Club (Hawkshill)   ★★★

Swailend, Newmacher, AB21 7UU
Nearest main town: Aberdeen

Secretary: Mr G. McIntosh   Tel: 01651 863002
                                            Fax: 01651 863055
Professional: Mr P. Smith   Tel: 01651 862127

Playing: Midweek: round £25.00; day £35.00. Weekend: round
                    £30.00; day £40.00. Handicap certificate required.

Facilities: Bar: 11am–11pm. Food: Lunch and dinner by arrange-
                    ment. Bar snacks.

Comments: Excellent layout and good mix of holes ... Superb home
                    stretch ... Dave Thomas design of considerable flair.

Newmacher Golf Club (Swailend)   ★★

Swailend, Newmacher, AB21 7UU
Nearest main town: Aberdeen

Secretary:	Mr G. McIntosh	Tel: 01651 863002
		Fax: 01651 863055
Professional:	Mr P. Smith	Tel: 01651 862127

Playing: Midweek: round £15.00; day £25.00. Weekend: round £30.00; day £30.00. Handicap certificate required.

Facilities: Bar: 11am–11pm. Food: Lunch and dinner by arrangement. Bar snacks.

Comments: Top course for one so young ... Newer than the Hawkshill and it shows ... Nice variety but wouldn't go back ... Other fish to fry in Scotland, I'm afraid.

Peterculter Golf Club ★★

Oldtown, Burnside Road, Peterculter, AB14 0LN
Nearest main town: Aberdeen

Secretary:	Mr K. Anderson	Tel: 01224 735245
		Fax: 01224 735580
Professional:	Mr D. Vannet	Tel: 01224 734994

Playing: Midweek: round £14.00; day £20.00. Weekend: round £17.00; day £23.00. Handicap certificate required.

Facilities: Bar: 11am–11pm. Food: Lunch and dinner from 10am–9pm, except Mondays.

Comments: Great greens – lots of birdies ... Lovely wildlife by the River Dee ... Narrow course and tough par ... Interesting holes, the pick is the 2nd.

Peterhead Golf Club ★★

Craigewan Links, Peterhead, AB42 1LT
Nearest main town: Aberdeen

Secretary:	Mr M. Sexton	Tel: 01779 472149
		Fax: 01779 480725
Professional:	None.	

Playing: Midweek: round £16.00; day £22.00. Weekend: round £20.00; day £27.00. Handicap certificate required.

Facilities: Bar: 11am–11pm. Food: Lunch from 10am–3pm. Dinner by arrangement.

Comments: Very basic facilities but course is good ... Natural delight ... Ditches, streams, bunkers and bushes ... A design that seems timeless ... Very intimidating in the wind ... Near to Cruden Bay, so combine the two.

Portlethen Golf Club   ★★★

Badentoy Road, Portlethen, AB12 4YA
Nearest main town: Aberdeen

Secretary:	None.	Tel: 01224 781090
		Fax: 01224 781090
Professional:	Mrs M. Thomson	Tel: 01224 782571

Playing: Midweek: round £14.00; day £21.00. Weekend: round £21.00; day £30.00. Handicap certificate required.

Facilities: Bar: 11am–11pm. Food: Lunch and dinner from 10am–10pm. Bar snacks.

Comments: Longish parkland course ... Worth popping in ... Good value ... Back nine a little tougher than front ... Four par-4s over 420 yards ... A long hitter's paradise.

Royal Aberdeen Golf Club   ★★★★

Balgownie, Bridge of Don, Aberdeen, AB23 8AT
Nearest main town: Aberdeen

Secretary:	Mr G. F. Webster	Tel: 01224 702571
		Fax: 01224 826591
Professional:	Mr R. MacAskill	Tel: 01224 702221

Playing: Midweek: round £55.00; day £75.00. Weekend: round £65.00; day n/a. Handicap certificate required.

Facilities: Bar: 11am–11pm. Food: Lunch from noon–3pm. Dinner by arrangement.

Comments: A forgotten links that is a privilege to play ... Inaccessible course that is so natural ... Bodies lurk in the rough here ... A treat for overseas visitors ... There's nothing else like it ... A classic of its type ... So much history here ... Where the game was born.

Royal Tarlair Golf Club   ★★

Buchan Street, Macduff, AB44 1TA
Nearest main town: Banff

Secretary: Mrs C. Davidson   Tel: 01261 832897
Professional: None.

Playing: Midweek: round £10.00; day £15.00. Weekend: round
                   £13.00; day £20.00. Handicap certificate required.

Facilities: Bar: 11am–11pm. Food: Lunch and dinner from
                   10am–9pm.

Comments: Superb views over the Moray Firth ... Cliff-top course,
                   very attractive ... One of the weakest Royal courses ...
                   Views the highlight of otherwise humdrum course.

Stonehaven Golf Club   ★★★

Cowie, Stonehaven, AB39 3RH
Nearest main town: Stonehaven

Secretary: Mr W. A. Donald   Tel: 01569 762124
                                          Fax: 01569 765973
Professional: None.

Playing: Midweek: round n/a; day £15.00. Weekend: round n/a;
                   day £20.00. Handicap certificate required.

Facilities: Bar: 11am–11pm. Food: Breakfast, lunch and dinner
                   from 9am–9pm. Bar snacks.

Comments: Very remote ... Short but a real battle ... Wish I'd never
                   turned up – too tough ... If you like a challenge ...
                   Seven par-3s ... At the mercy of the elements, as golf
                   should be.

Strathlene Golf Club   ★★

Buckie, AB5 2DJ
Nearest main town: Buckie

Secretary: To be appointed.   Tel: 01542 831798
Professional: None.

Playing: Midweek: round £12.00; day £18.00. Weekend: round
                   £16.00; day £20.00. Handicap certificate required.

Facilities: Bar: 11am–11pm. Food: Bar snacks.

Comments: Excellent value seaside course ... Plenty of elevated greens ... Always felt part of the club, even as a visitor ... Didn't mind leaving ... Wind plays havoc here.

Index of Courses

Aberdour 51
Aboyne 102
Alloa 51
Alyth 87
Arbroath 88
Auchterarder 88

Baberton 60
Balbirnie Park 51
Ballater 102
Ballochmyle 14
Belleisle 15
Blairgowrie (Lansdowne) 89
Blairgowrie (Rosemount) 89
Boat of Garten 75
Bothwell Castle 15
Braehead 90
Braemar 103
Braid Hills 60
Brechin 90
Broomieknowie 61
Brora 75
Brunston Castle 16
Bruntsfield Links 61
Buchanan Castle 90

Callander 91
Camperdown 91
Cardross 16
Carnegie 76
Carnoustie 85
Carnoustie Burnside 92
Carradale 17
Cathcart Castle 17
Cathkin Braes 18
Cawder 18
Cochrane Castle 18
Cowglen 19
Crail 52
Crieff 92
Crow Wood 19
Cruden Bay 101
Cullen 103

Dalmilling 20
Deer Park CC 62
Deeside 104
Downfield 93
Drumoig 52
Drumpelier 20
Duddingston 62
Duff House Royal 104
Dullatur 21
Dumfries & Country 42
Dunbar 62
Dunfermline 53
Duns 42

East Renfrewshire 21
Edzell 93
Elderslie 22
Elgin 76
Erskine 22

Forfar 94
Forres 77
Fortrose and Rosemarkie 77
Fraserburgh 104

Girvan 23
Glasgow 24
Glasgow Gailes 23
Gleddoch 24
Glenbervie 54
Glencruitten 25
Gleneagles Hotel (King's) 86
Gleneagles Hotel (Monarch) 99
Gleneagles Hotel (Queens) 100
Golf House Club 54
Golspie 78
Gourock 25
Grantown-on-Spey 79
Green Hotel 94
Greenburn 63
Gullane (No. 1) 64
Gullane (No. 2) 64
Gullane (No. 3) 64

Haddington 65
Haggs Castle 26
Hawick 43
Hayston 26
Hazelhead 105
Hilton Park 26
Hopeman 78
Huntly 105

Invergordon 79
Inverness 80-81
Irvine 27

Kemnay 106
Kilmacolm 27
Kilmarnock 28
Kilspindie 65
King James VI 95
King's Links 106
Kings Acre 66
Kingsbarns 47
Kingussie 80
Kintore 107
Kirkcaldy 55
Kirkhill 28
Kirriemuir 95

Ladybank 48
Lanark 28
Largs 29
Letham Grange 96
Leven Links 55
Liberton 66
Loch Lomond 29
Lochranza 30
Lochwinnoch 30
Longniddry 67
Lothianburn 67
Loudoun Gowf 30
Luffness 67
Lundin 56

Machrie Hotel 31
Machrihanish 31
Marriott Dalmahoy Hotel 68
Millport 32

Milngavie 32
Moffat 43
Monifieth (Ashludie) 96
Monifieth (Medal) 96
Montrose 97
Moray (New) 81
Moray (Old) 80
Mortonhall 68
Muir of Ord 33
Muirfield 60
Murcar 107
Murrayshall Hotel 97
Musselburgh 69

Nairn 81
Nairn Dunbar 81
Newburgh-on-Ythan 108
Newmacher (Hawkshill) 108
Newmacher (Swailend) 108
Newton Stewart 43
Newtonmore 82
North Berwick 69

Paisley 33
Panmure 98
Peebles 44
Peterculter 109
Peterhead 109
Pitlochry 98
Pitreavie (Dunfermline) 56
Pollock 33
Port Glasgow 34
Portlethen 110
Portpatrick 44
Powfoot 45
Prestonfield 70
Prestwick 34
Prestwick St Cuthbert 35
Prestwick St Nicholas 35

Ralston 35
Ranfurly Castle 36
Ratho Park 70
Roxburghe 45
Royal Aberdeen 110
Royal Burgess 71

Royal Dornoch 74
Royal Musselburgh 71
Royal Tarlair 111
Royal Troon 11

Scotscraig 56
Shiskine 36
Southerness 41
St Andrews (Jubilee) 57
St Andrews (New) 58
St Andrews (Old) 49
St Andrews Eden 57
Stirling 99
Stonehaven 111
Stranraer 46
Strathaven 37
Strathlene 111
Strathpeffer Spa 82

Tain 83
Taymouth Castle 99
The Dukes 53
The Glen 71
Traigh Golf Course 83
Troon Portland 37
Turnberry Hotel (Ailsa) 12
Turnberry Hotel (Arran) 38

Vale of Leven 38

West Kilbride 39
West Linton 72
West Lothian 72
Western Gailes 13
Westerwood Hotel 39
Whitekirk 73
Wick 84
Windyhill 39